How to Get What You Want from Your Man Anytime

Introduction

Now you can get what you want from your man anytime—even when you have been frustrated by this man forever!

This book presents a step-by-step strategy that will teach you how to ask for what you want in such a way that your man will hear you. My goal is for you to have more fun, more sex, and less conflict in your intimate relationships.

I believe that everyone wants a relationship that is loving, affectionate, and satisfying. Do you remember when you first fell in love? Didn't everything feel wonderful, loving, and exciting? Remember how you couldn't stand to be separated? After years of togetherness, however, that craving you had for each other has probably lessened or you wouldn't be reading this book. Of course, you still love each other, but somehow there isn't that quickening of your pulse rate or the anticipation of touch that fuels your desires these days.

So what happened? Life happened. Everyday chores, children, work, bills, all of the challenges that make life what it is, have managed to interfere with the romance that created those titillating moments of anticipation.

For some of you who have yet to experience those feelings of being head-over-heels in love with someone, this book is for you, too.

Over the past 14 years since my separation and divorce, I've discovered a point of view or a strategy as I call it that really works for getting both men and women exactly what it is they most want out of their intimate relationship. From the comments my clients have made during the years that I've been a relationship coach, it has been validated over and over again that passion can survive family crises, and that men and women can love each other and satisfy each other's needs without bickering, nagging or arguing. It all depends on just a few crucial elements that you can easily learn if you are willing to look at a man/woman relationship from a slightly different point of view. To illustrate, let me tell you a little st

Through my relationship coaching busir   55 year old woman who had been married to the same mai   1

Acknowledgements

I'd like to acknowledge my daughters: Samantha, Cydney and Stephanie for being my joyous reason for living; their respective significant others: Jason, Geoff and Jason, who are even better than real sons because I'm not their mother, for their participation in my in-house laboratory.

I'm thankful for my grandchildren: Justin, Zakhary, and Jordan for being the ultimate pleasures in my life today and great child role models for distinctions in the sexes.

My gratitude and appreciation go to my delightful and loving friend and editor, Candace, for being so positive, so knowledgeable, so tenacious, and so empowering to me.

To my dedicated and objective personal coach, Faith, who has contributed to my life in innumerable ways and managed to keep my entrepreneurial brain focused long enough to finish this project.

To my wonderful friend, Maria, for having the strength of character to ask me for coaching when she still disliked me and for being willing to do whatever it took to get her results.

To Maria, Christine and Shanna, for their faith in me and my ideas, and for being so honest about their lives.

To my friend, Scott, for his always unwavering opinion and male perspective. Thank you for your unconditional honesty.

To Jack Rafferty for opening my eyes to what is possible in the way of relationship through his courses about men and women.

To Carlos Ochoa and Craig Vilaubi, for their beautiful graphic translations of my thoughts for the cover.

Finally, to each of my current and former clients for trusting me enough to share their intimate challenges and who took great risks with their hearts. Their successes have absolutely validated the theory in this book.

Contents

Dedication

I dedicate this book to the late Robert Mead Sheppard (1939-1999).

How to Get What You Want from Your Man Anytime

By

Susan Sheppard

particularly charming man, and in fact, he could sometimes be rather abusive. Over time, the man became very ill and died. His wife, call her Rosa, had been working two full-time night jobs for many years so that she could care for him in the daytime and pay all of his medical bills.

A few years after his death, Rosa decided that she really didn't like her life very much. All she did was work and she was really quite lonely. She came to me and told me that she wanted to get married again. However, this time, she wanted to marry someone who would take care of her. Rosa wasn't the most beautiful woman on the planet, but she was very sweet, sincere, and loving. She initially fixed her attention on a man who was her own age, but he didn't even know she was alive.

This took a little work, but she finally realized it wasn't getting her anywhere. We spent some time buying her more attractive clothes and lingerie. She learned how to apply makeup, and she was finally focusing on working less so she could have a balanced life.

Since Rosa was determined to do whatever it took to get what she wanted, she was willing to stretch her comfort zone and take some risks. I told her to meet forty men and decide what it was that she liked and disliked about each of them.

To get her started into the world of dating, she had some glamour photos taken, and then placed an ad in the personals. It wasn't long before she was very busy answering a ton of ads and giving responses.

From where she started to the eventual outcome, took about a year, and her story was amazing. As she began to meet men, her self-esteem increased, and each time that occurred, better quality men started showing up. The result was that she met a charming and wonderful widowed man, who was about her same age, with the same interests, and guess what else? He absolutely adored her.

Within a year, he took her to Paris for New Years and proposed at the Eiffel Tower. As it turned out, she got much more than she expected. It seems that he was quite well off with investments and property, so right now, she still works, but only ten days a month because that's her preference. He recently took early retirement, so the rest of the time they travel together, go to plays, art exhibits and are building two houses on the beach property he owned on the West Coast. They are both quite happy.

What happened to her seemed like a miracle, and it can happen to you, too. All you have to do is apply the same principles and strategies I taught her.

In the past 14 years, I have successfully coached men and women in all types of relationships and circumstances. I have worked with couples in relationships that were completely on the rocks, but who turned their situations around.

This book will show you how to rekindle your relationship and even teach you how to take that first step towards creating a relationship that's fun, fulfilling, and that works!

How To Get What You Want from Your Man Anytime! Reveals the easiest, most effective way to get satisfaction from a relationship—regardless of your love life's current condition.

- If you are married and you're struggling to stay married . . .

- If you are married and you just want more pleasure . . .

- If you are married and thinking you can't stand it anymore . . .

- If you are married and you're bored with your partner . . .

- If you are married and think your spouse is cheating . . .

- If you are married and wondering is this all there is . . .

OR

- If you are divorced, widowed or separated and don't have a clue how to reenter the relationship world . . .

OR

- If you are single and have been dating whoever shows up . . .

- If you are single and haven't been on a date in years . . .

- If you are single and feel undesirable . . .

- If you are single and don't have a clue where to start . . .

- If you are single and want to get married . . .

Then this book is for you.

It doesn't matter how old you are, how long you have been looking, how many times you have tried in the past, or what you have learned about relationships from your friends and family—this strategy can work for you.

Here are a few examples of what you can expect to find in this book:

- Determining what women really want

- Discovering what men really want

- How to figure out what it is that you really want

- How to ask for what you want in a way that you will be heard

- How to find your perfect mate

- How to keep sex hot

- How to talk to each other about anything

- How to avoid what happens to most marriages that don't work

- Discover the secret to achieving sacred intimacy

- How to avoid settling for less than what you want

Before you begin learning about my relationship strategy, I want to make it perfectly clear that I am not a therapist, a psychologist, a marriage counselor, or a psychic. I have been coaching men and women in relationships for the past fourteen years with remarkable results. The people who are most successful hiring me as their coach are those who are willing to do whatever it takes to get their results. I believe that if you want positive results that are different from what you've been getting, then you must employ different actions.

This book provides specific steps for entering or achieving a relationship that works. It's about having fun, being in love, and having a relationship where everyone wins and gets satisfaction. It's a controversial strategy, certainly not the only strategy, but one that over the past fourteen years has brought amazing results into my clients' lives. It is at their request that I have written this book to share my knowledge and strategy for getting what you want from your man anytime. If you are open to looking at a strategy that might change your entire perception about what the man/woman relationship is, then this is a concept that could change your life forever.

What I'd like you to do is to suspend everything that you believe is true about marriage, love, and relationship. Be willing to test the theory and use it yourself. If you doubt the concept, that is okay, just look at your own relationship. If you are getting absolutely everything you want from each other, and you have a powerful, exciting, sexually-fulfilling relationship, then don't change a thing. However, if you aren't getting everything you want from your relationship, you might want to consider changing your mind. Consider experimenting with this strategy and then take a risk by practicing the concepts as described in this book. They might surprise you.

Disclaimer #1: I have chosen not to include references to gay couples in this book. My experience with coaching gay couples is non-existent so far; therefore, I don't believe my own credibility in reference to gay relationships. Someone with experience in coaching gay couples may find the concepts applicable.

Disclaimer #2: Many generalizations are stated within this book for presenting a concept. These statements are not intended to categorize, judge, or limit any person of either sex.

Are you ready to begin?

Chapter 1
The Strategy for Having a Successful Male-Female Relationship

"The only place that women have ultimate power is in a relationship. It is the woman's job to provide the appetite for pleasure. To express appetite, the woman must have self-esteem and know what she wants. Then she must ask for it in a way that her man can hear her."

—Susan Sheppard
How to Get What You Want from Your Man Anytime

Confusion within a relationship exists when a woman displays a lack of clarity for what she wants from her man. Specifically, when she constantly hints at what she really wants instead of asking for it, the man becomes frustrated. Women are so used to taking care of everyone else's needs that when it comes to their own, they rarely define what it is that they want. They get a sense about something and then hint about it to their man, who since his goal is to please his woman; then tries to produce the result.

The outcome of these shenanigans is that the woman gets angry with her man for not knowing what it is that she wants, when she never really asked for it in the first place. So, what is the core issue of this confusion and how can she really know what she wants? She must recognize that she has all the power in the relationship, and that she must make it her priority to delve into her own wants and needs to clarify what exactly it is that she wants. Once that is established, it then becomes her responsibility to request exactly what it is that she wants from her man who will then produce it for her.

Scenario: Confusion within a Relationship

Let's look at an example of ambiguity and confusion within a relationship. Katie and Kevin have been dating for a few weeks. The following argument takes place in Kevin's car, while they're trying to decide where to have dinner.

Kevin

What do you want to eat?

Katie

I don't know. What do you want? (Actually, she does know but she thinks it isn't appropriate for her to say.)

Kevin

You get to choose. I'm taking you out. (He wants to please her.)

Katie

I had Chinese for lunch. (She'd really like Italian, maybe some lasagna, but she's afraid he will think she is too fat and shouldn't eat lasagna.)

Kevin

So you don't want Chinese then. (Stating the obvious and waiting for a clue.)

Katie

No, what do you feel like having? (Hoping he will come up with a suggestion of Italian.)

Kevin

I don't care. I could eat at McDonald's. (He really doesn't care. He's just hungry.)

Katie

I don't want to go to McDonald's. (Insulted because she now thinks he thinks she is a cheap date and he can just take her to McDonald's.)

Kevin

Well, where do you want to go?

Katie

I told you. I don't care. (She still thinks she wants Lasagna from an Italian restaurant.)

Kevin

But you seem to care since you don't want Chinese or McDonald's. (He's starting to get frustrated.)

Katie

Why do we always have to have this argument? Can't you just pick a nice place to take me so we can just enjoy ourselves? (She wants him to read her mind and pick the place she wants to go without her having to say it.)

Kevin

I just want to take you somewhere that you want to go. (He's not a mind reader.)

Katie

Why can't you be the man and surprise me? (Still hoping he will suggest Italian.)

Kevin

All right then, we will go to the Thirty-Fiver for burgers. (At least he can get a beer and there might be some of his buddies there because this date is getting to be a drag.)

Katie

I hate that place; it's so gross and loud. (She doesn't want a burger. She already said no to McDonald's.)

Kevin

Well, how about suggesting something that you really want? (He's still trying to please her.)

Katie

Why do I always have to decide? You never want to go where I suggest anyway. We always have to do what you want to do. (Realizing they are now arguing and she still isn't getting what she wants.)

Kevin

I am trying to get you to tell me what you really want to eat, but fine, I'll decide. (He's angry now.) We are going to Dave's Steakhouse. It's a nice sit-down restaurant and you can order anything you want from a quesadilla to a steak dinner.

Katie

That's a nice place but isn't it a little far away and I'm not dressed to go there. I'm hungry now and you just don't care about me.

Kevin

(He stops the car.) Fine! I'm not driving anywhere until you pick what you want to eat. Here are your choices. Burgers are out. Chinese is out. Dave's is out. What's left, a salad, Mexican, Thai, sushi, pizza, or hot dogs from the push cart? What do you want?

Katie

How about pizza? (She's thinking he will finally come up with an Italian restaurant that she likes. Kevin starts driving again.)

Kevin

Fine. Here's Domino's (He pulls into the parking lot and stops the car.)

Katie

Fine. (She is pouting however, because she really wanted to go to Casa Palazzo where they have a great antipasto salad and the lasagna that she wanted in the first place.)

Kevin

Are you happy now? (He is frustrated and irritated because he still knows that she is not happy with his choice, but he never figured out what she really wanted.)

Scenario Analysis

This is a slightly exaggerated version of a common interchange that occurs between couples. Almost every person has participated in a similar conversation at some time in his or her intimate relationship. What happened in this scenario is typical of the confusion that occurs in relationships. The woman does not have the self-esteem to ask for what she wants. She is afraid that he will criticize her choice or shoot it down. Therefore, she lives in hope that he will accidentally discover what she wants. This is the reason men get frustrated and say that women don't know what they want. This is also the reason that women get frustrated and say that men don't care about what they want. There is a part of her that believes that he should know what she wants without her having to say so.

A Woman's Role within a Relationship

A woman's station in life for millions of years has been to be the partner of a man, the rejuvenator, the nurturer, and the source of her man's success. In ancient times, tribal customs dictated the death of a woman who was not successful at finding a man to take care of her. It is instinct that propels a woman to find a man and marry him, bear children, and have an appetite for sex, motherhood, nurturing, and love.

Therefore, when a woman does not have a man of her own, or a family of her own, the underlying inference is that she can't get one, which ultimately is disgraceful to her and her family and this causes direct damage to her self-esteem. In modern times, during the past 100 years, women have emerged as self-sufficient and successful in business. Has this improved a woman's self-esteem? In terms of relationship, it really hasn't, because it is instinctual for her to want a man in her life or else she doesn't feel complete.

Very subtle, other-than-conscious anger at the world for not allowing her to be equal, domination by men and government (mainly men) and church (mainly men) and business (mainly men) have perpetuated a second-class citizen belief for women. Frustration abounds because she cannot be in the men's club, the good old boys network, and that she must work twice as hard and be twice as smart to compete in the man's world. It is what drives woman's vengeance on man.

The Male-Female Relationship

Have you noticed that a woman will show meanness to the man she loves? Until she knows that she can trust him not to leave her, she will be charming and nice. Once she begins to trust him, she can show him her mean streak. This sounds ridiculous, however, it is only when a woman is sure that a man loves her that she will nag him, be sarcastic with him, and treat him with disdain when he does not perform to her standards. This inherent meanness arises from millions of years of domination by men. It is instinctual and referred to by men as the nagging wife persona.

Let's look at the male-female love relationship from another perspective. What if the sexual act is a metaphor for relationship and how it works? If this theory were true, then men who produce erections are about production, and women who receive the erection from their men are about appetite. There is some logic to this, but what does it mean in regards to relationship?

It's important to recognize that male-female relationships exist because men and women are physically different and that we were created to be two parts of a whole and are only complete when joined. Let's assume that this is true. Then, what if we are emotionally and psychologically just as different and yet still created to be two parts of a whole in every way? Next, imagine we are destined to meet, mate and create an energy cycle that can escalate to a peak or disintegrate with a thud.

What if we are supposed to spend our lives on this earth searching for, finding and eventually mating with that other part of us? What if disintegration occurs when the energies are not compatible and when the energies compliment each other, the reaction increases and the demand for more energy escalates as each partner experiences higher attraction? With that, each person's self-esteem is boosted.

What happens when you combine self-esteem with attraction and energy? Is love created? If all of the above assumptions could be true, then what I am about to describe to you could also be a very fresh perspective in which we examine the male-female relationship. This is my invitation to you to look with new eyes at love and relationship.

Through coaching hundreds of individuals and couples, I have learned that contempt arises when the system fails. The entire system creates a cycle, which can either ascend or descend. The ascending cycle expands to create love, affection, and eventually sex. The descending cycle is accompanied by mistrust, disrespect, a judgmental attitude, and eventually if left to deteriorate, contempt.

Understanding the Ascending Cycle of Relationship

This whole concept recognizes that an ascending cycle is created when a man performs so that a woman will notice him. Here's the process:

- The woman notices and chooses to test the man

- The man wants to please the woman

- The woman approves of the man

- The man increases his attention to the woman

- The woman acknowledges his production

- The woman asks for what she wants

- The man produces what she wants

- The woman approves of his production and acknowledges movement in the direction she wants the relationship to go.

Understanding the Descending Cycle of Relationship

In a descending cycle, both participants suffer from diminished self-esteem, but for different reasons. Let's look at what happened in my former marriage. When my husband and I married, we were at the peak of the ascending cycle. It went downhill from that point. Before our three children were born, I told him that he could do what he wanted in relation to work and not to worry about making money, because I could do that. He took my words literally and did what he wanted to do, which was to work as a wrestling coach for kids—for free.

As a result, he didn't contribute to the marriage with a weekly paycheck. As our family grew, I became very resentful and angry at having to support all of us. He continued to do his coaching thing and the longer he persisted, the more I believed that he couldn't do anything else. I lost respect for him as a provider and then he did even less. Therefore, the cycle was reversed.

We eventually divorced and it was only then that I started to learn how relationships worked. The catalyst in both the ascending and descending cycles is self-esteem. When it starts downward, each person starts to lose a little self-esteem and thinks that they don't deserve to have better. As the journey continues, it gets worse. The woman in this example, "me," decided it was because I was not attractive enough. The man generally will decide that he cannot produce the results that his wife wants and his self-esteem deteriorates.

Men are Linear Thinkers and Results-Oriented

Let's take a moment and look at how a man approaches most situations. I believe that men are linear thinkers, primarily left brained, and they think logically. They like to make things work. Wherever men are, you will find games, gadgets, problems, and work. Even their play is competitive, such as golf, tennis, or video games. In addition, watching television isn't good enough without the remote. Men measure everything and compete everywhere. I have watched men create a pool for money betting on how long one of their friends will stay married.

The fact that men are solution-oriented is obvious by the reality that anytime a woman starts to tell any man about a situation, the first thing that he will do is start to offer solutions. A man will tell her how to fix the problem even when the woman has not asked for a solution. Usually, all she really wants is someone to listen to her. Men, for the most part, are more interested in the bottom-line results of a project than how to get there. They think in a production way. Even in sex, men believe that their job is to produce an erection or the sex can't get done.

Driven by Instincts

Driven by their instincts to reach a solitary goal, men, being linear thinkers, rely on logic, and are extremely results-oriented. They can only do one thing at a time. For example, think about a teenage boy and his goal on a date. His goal is to score. Therefore, he focuses on that one seemingly unattainable goal. He takes a shower, dresses in clean and sharp-looking clothes as defined by a woman. He washes his car to make him look good. He brings flowers. He's polite to her parents, and takes her dancing just to please her, although he hates it.

All his actions are driven by his hope that his date will allow him to look at, brush against, and possibly touch those beautiful fantasy items he has in his mind called breasts. To him, that is the goal. He has no thoughts of relationship, being a boyfriend, taking the relationship to a committed level, or anything else except the thought of getting a little feel and possibly scoring sexually. We see this again in the boy's locker room at school on Monday when one can hear many stories of sexual exploits and scores that never happened.

Consider this next example to illustrate the contrast between male unidimensional goal-oriented thinking and the female's circular, random thinking. A man and woman take a weekend, getaway trip on a state highway going from Los Angeles to San Francisco. The man will boast that he can make the trip in only six hours. Most women that I know would prefer to take the coast highway and stop along the way for an intimate dinner or even for sex at a beautiful place. In fact, most women probably wouldn't mind losing their direction and ending up somewhere else entirely, as long as it was romantic.

Men are results-oriented. It starts when they are little boys playing T-ball for the fun of the game, but by the end of their first season, they are already competitive, wanting to know who won, what's the score, and getting angry with themselves if they miss a play or don't get a hit. They don't allow themselves space to make mistakes.

Certainly, you've heard the expression that if a man doesn't know where he is going, he will not stop and ask for directions. Why? Well, it appears that it would make him look like less of a man. His goal is to get where he is going and even if he doesn't know where that is, he will make up his mind that he knows.

One more extremely important validation of being results-oriented lies in the act of making love. A young, inexperienced man's goal is orgasm, his own and hopefully though not always, his partner's. It is rare to find a man who can actually enjoy the journey, the pleasure of touch and sensuality without finally reaching his goal of orgasm. Even while focusing on his partner's pleasure, his ultimate goal then becomes her orgasm, and he cannot feel successful if she does not achieve that.

Instinctive behavior for men is an aggressive attitude. It is genetic and arises from millions of years of dominant, territorial behavior. In the animal world, males fight over territory, females, and food. Bullies abound in the young, human male culture. I read once that every man can name the bully who terrorized him when he was in third grade. Test it. Ask one.

All men are macho. They cannot help themselves, and in fact, it is one of the most endearing characteristics and an attractive quality in a man, as long as he has a sensitive side to him as well.

Many men claim to be "enlightened men" as they brag about supporting women in their independence. However, in most cases, it's an act. I still believe that all men are inherently macho and those enlightened males have simply discovered that enlightenment will get them to their scoring position a lot quicker than doing the standard macho act.

Boys are raised from the time of birth to suck it up, be a man, get over it, be tough, etc. Today, it's easy to observe young parents automatically encourage their little boys to be brave and tough it out instead of crying when they get hurt.

The fear of having a wimpy son is too great to let the boy be emotional and express his pain. Boys therefore learn macho at a very young age and accept that they must look tough even if they don't feel it. They learn early that if they display weakness anywhere, their buddies will tease them, their fathers will encourage them to get tough, and even their mothers will tell them, "You're not hurt, get up and play some more." This is the origin of macho. It comes under the guise of looking good for a man.

Male Dominance

Evidence overwhelms us that men have always dominated women. I know lots of women out there who see themselves as liberated and self-sufficient and will debate this point, but look around. How many women are in Congress, the Senate, the Presidency, or the vice-president's chair in the United States?

For that matter, how many women are CEOs of major companies? How many women are high-ranking officers in the military? How many women produce and direct major motion pictures? How many women run construction companies? How many women are self-made multi-billionaires? Okay, there are a lot more women in all of those positions than there has ever been in the past, but in the big scheme of things, how many women really rule anything except a family and their own personal business?

It is my belief that the mind-set against women being in power is so pervasive and so accepted that we don't even recognize it. Women are so pre-conditioned to accept second-class citizenship that most times it goes unnoticed. It is only when a woman is singled out and recognized, and achieves a position of power that anyone actually notices by comparison that most women are still where they always were. Things are changing, but very slowly.

This book is not about the woman's plight in the world. Nor is this book intended to undermine the greatness or attractiveness of men. Why I even mention this is to create the foundation for what drives relationships in our current world. Underneath all the stereotypes, lies the fact that men have more physical strength than women do. Ultimately, women recognize men's physical dominance. They harbor a fear of potential violence from the dark side of men, those unknown to them or even those men who are in familiar relationships when things deteriorate and turn ugly.

Women Enhance the Quality of Life

A woman always enhances the quality of life. In fact, their responsibility in life is to guide the direction of their family. More basic than that is that a woman is the vessel in which the seed of humanity grows to fruition. Women are the counterpart to a man. They bear their children, nurse them through childhood, and provide a home and security for the family as it grows. A woman cannot bear a child without the man's sperm. They are physically less strong and yet in so many ways stronger than the man.

In the metaphor of sex as relationship, women receive the male organs inside their body and receive the sperm for fertilization. So in looking at the relationship, they are also in the receiving position. In ages gone by, they were the homemakers, the child nurturer; they were the comfort for the man returning home from hunting. Women even were the ones who discovered farming so they could keep their men home.

Women are Creative and Non-Linear Circular Thinkers

In contrast to the male, women are creative and non-linear circular thinkers. Women find pleasure in the journey sometimes even more than the results. In this context, it is the woman's responsibility to claim her power in the relationship and to express her appetite to her man so that he can better provide for her and their family. I believe that in following through on this metaphor, "it is the woman's job to express her appetite" and have it "be" more than the man thinks he can produce, and to believe in his ability to produce that result until he does it. This is where a man gets to express his dreams, and his woman can encompass them into her appetite. Their relationship is the catalyst for breathing life into their dreams.

Knowing what is actually going on in your relationship and sensing the truth is a skill that women possess due to their innate intuitiveness. Women are multidimensional in their abilities. They are able to perform several simultaneous tasks (hand a snack to a toddler, supervise homework, kiss a husband hello, talk on the phone and respond appropriately to three different questions). In addition, they can comprehend the emotional temperature of each exchange and do all of this while they are making dinner.

These skills validate a woman's unique abilities and prove her superiority in the intuitive realm.

A woman knows more about what is happening in a relationship at any given time than a man will ever know. Women are relationship-oriented. They are creative in ways that can solve confrontations in non-violent ways. Women learn to express their emotions rather than suppress them.

Little girls are protected from violence by their fathers and big brothers. Because of the way they are dressed as children and the way they are raised, they don't get into the same kind of situations that boys do. They are taught to be ladies, to be polite, to look pretty, and to be gracious. They are allowed to cry. Not to say that girls don't get dirty and compete or get aggressive, they do. Girls, however, grow up differently than boys. There are plenty of girl bullies in third grade; but girls learn to manipulate and to hurt other girls in non-violent, non-physical ways. Girls learn to be verbally aggressive and penetrating. Girls grow up ignorant of the fact that boys do not have the same ability to intuit, create, and verbally spar. Therefore, one of a woman's greatest weaknesses is the assumption that men have the same abilities as women when it comes to relating as human beings and intuitively knowing.

Dumbness on the part of men is one reason why women must ask for what they want. A man I know described his biggest frustration about his girlfriend in this way: "I could tell that I did something wrong by the expression on her face. That clue prompted me to ask her what was wrong. I knew I had done something but I didn't have any idea what it was. Her response: 'If you don't know I'm not going to tell you' only dumfounded me further.'"

Men require direction because they really are ignorant about what women want and how they think. Men truly want to please women but they honestly don't know how. Women, coming from scarcity, do not know how to accurately describe their wants (appetite) and be direct in requesting them (placing orders).

Getting Clarity about What You Want

One of a woman's jobs in relationship is to get clarity about what she wants. Have it be more than what the man in her life thinks that he can produce, and ask for it in a way that proves to him that she believes, no matter what, that he will produce that result for her. I know that this is contrary to what most women have been raised to do, but I have proof. I have validation that this is what makes a relationship work. It is what brings passion and power to a relationship. It is what will change our world. Women must be honest with themselves first, about what it is they want, and then they must be gut-level honest with their men and place an order as if from a menu for what they want.

Reassurance that he is the provider and the producer in the family allows the man in the relationship to be a man. It's her approval of him and belief in him, which causes their self-esteem to rise. A relationship thrives when a woman approves of her man. She trusts that he will produce for her. She knows that when she orders something from the menu of life that this man who loves her, partly because she approves of him and believes in him, will climb mountains, crawl over broken glass and hot coals to prove to her that he is the man she believes him to be. This is where the macho in men motivates them to produce the impossible results.

This is where the idea of "a woman behind the man" originated. It seems hokey but what we are looking at is five million years of instinctive behavior versus a hundred years of technology that has attempted to even the score for women. Fighting these instincts is futile. A woman doesn't have to become a helpless manipulative female to do this. On the contrary, she can be as powerful and successful as she wants to be. She just needs to recognize that she needs her man to be a man and allow him to prove it to her. She needs to stop competing with him. A woman's power is in her femininity not in trying to be as macho as he is.

How to Expand Your Appetite to Get What You Want

Asking for what you want, approving of your man's production and appreciation for his efforts in achieving your orders is what causes the upward spiral of this strategy on love and relationship. Everyone wins. Women are happy because not only have they figured out what they want, but also they have asked for and received it from someone they love. Men are happy because they are able to please their women. They achieve something they didn't believe that they could, and overall, everyone's self-esteem escalates. This is the magic of love. Everyone wins because everyone is playing the game by the same rules. I know it sounds excessively simple; however, the proof is in the testing.

Here is what has to happen to make a relationship work, and we haven't even approached the subject of sex yet:

- Women have to stop being mean

- Men have to surrender to a woman's power to lead the relationship

- They both have to approve of each other, be straight, ask for what they want and exuberantly appreciate the other's efforts to produce.

The "How to Get What You Want from Your Man Anytime" Strategy

- Be direct.

- Acknowledge him graciously and honestly.

- Use your appetite to ask for EXACTLY what you want.

- Ignore his hesitation and objections because men always say no at first. If he doesn't say no, be wary of him telling you what you want to hear just to get what he wants (sex).

- Recognize when he violates one of your MAJOR standards and never settle.

- When he produces the result you want, show your appreciation.

- Dismiss him completely when he doesn't produce for you.

Chapter 2

Dating Helps Expand Your Limits and Boundaries

"A man of self-esteem . . . feels an intense need to find human beings he can admire—to find a spiritual equal whom he can love. The quality that will attract him most is self-esteem . . . ."
—Ayn Rand, *The Virtue of Selfishness*

We define dating as an engagement to go out socially with another person, often out of romantic interest. Traditionally, dating is known as a pastime for the adolescent and young adult communities. To me, it has always been something we did in high school and college. For terminology's sake, anyone over 30 can be seeing someone, involved, engaged, living together or just going out. For anyone older than 40, it has always seemed odd to hear them say, "My boyfriend," or "I'm dating a lot of men."

Mature people seem to float in and out of relationships, and a serious commitment is a forgotten goal. However, when people re-enter the relationship search, regardless of their age, dating feels awkward and somehow trivial. Desiring a common bond with someone of the opposite sex, and then progressing to romance and possibly commitment, demands that you expand your limits and boundaries.

I tell all my clients, no matter what their age, that they need to start from the beginning and re-define the traits and values that they find attractive because it will not be the same for everyone. Women who are looking for a husband always seem hungry and needy. Women who are expanding their comfort zone, meeting, and exploring many new people appear to be a lot more intriguing.

It is a known fact that if you aren't attached, then you aren't afraid of losing. It's a whole lot easier to dismiss a man who doesn't meet your standards when you aren't grasping at him as if he were the last available man on earth. The media and those well-known colloquialisms, such as: "It's easier to . . . than it is to find a man when you are over 30" have perpetuated "coming from scarcity," where men are concerned. Personally, I think that is a lot of nonsense.

You can find a man who meets your standards if you decide you want to and you are willing to do whatever it takes. My strategy is that you must be determined not to crumble under the stress of asking for what you want and then hold out until you get it! There are plenty of available men. You just have to be willing to meet quite a few until you're ready to recognize the one you truly want; the one who exhibits the qualities and behavior that proves he deserves to have you.

Setting the Boundaries for Finding Your Dream Man

To find your dream man when you are serious about wanting a committed relationship, just follow the steps below, and then apply my strategy.

1. Visualize the perfect mate for yourself. Get very specific. Be sure to include the values and principals that mean the most to you. Write it all down in a list. It's important that you don't forget anything because whatever you forget will show up in the next man who tries to date you. One extremely important element if you really want a relationship is to require that a man is ready, available, and willing to be in a relationship. Otherwise, the person who arrives will probably be married or under 18.

2. When you've completed your written list, choose a date by which you want to meet this person and then file the list away or post it on one of the dream realization Web sites, such as www.dreamroundup.com. By doing these things, you have sent a message out to the universe and requested assistance from a higher power. [Be realistic about the month and date. Asking for a man to show up

next week is unrealistic if you want to apply the strategy I am about to teach you.]

3. Forget about "the list" and go about your life, making sure to take care of yourself in an extraordinary manner.

4. Next on the agenda: I want you to meet *forty* new men. Yes, that is not a typo. I said 40. Notice that I did not say "date" forty new men. You can have a meaningful conversation, become friends, and ask questions about what is attractive to them. If you persist past 10 new men, you will notice a change in the type of men you are meeting; go past 20 and you will notice a change in yourself and what you expect from men. Beyond 30, be prepared to meet the person of your dreams, because shortly after the date that you designated on your "list," you will notice that there is a person in your life who fits the description that you specified. Caution: He still may not be the one. More about this later.

5. Waiting until that man gets around to asking you out can take awhile, especially if you don't communicate your interests and intentions. Once you meet your dream man, you can directly ask him to be in a relationship with you. Contrary to all popular opinion, my suggestion is to be straight about what you want from a man. It's not meant to scare him away, just to declare your intentions. If the man gets scared and runs, he probably was not the one that you wanted and he didn't deserve to be in a relationship with you anyway.

6. Flirting with a man also works if you are honest and open and ask for what you want. None of the above applies if you are just looking for a date, someone to play with or if you are a teenager.

7. You must go out with a lot of frogs before you find your prince. Widen your expectations. Expand your horizons. Broaden your comfort zone. Don't always limit yourself to the people you think are exactly what you want. You will be surprised who you are attracted to and will consider as a life mate when you get to know him better.

Dating in the Workplace

A conflict of interests is a good way of describing the state of affairs when you are dating someone with whom you work. Moods change, and personal feelings interfere with productivity. It's difficult to discipline or fire someone whose toes you have been sucking. That's a little overboard, but when work is impacted by personal relationships, it affects everyone in the department. It isn't just the two people involved who feel the affects of a disagreement or the attraction energy. Please don't ever think that you can keep it a secret. The pheromones alone announce it better than neon flashing lights when you date a co-worker, boss, or employee.

Fraudulent Dating

Fraud in dating is a significant issue. Married people have a tendency to lie about their status when they are pursuing someone in a new relationship. DUH! Appreciation for honesty is manifested when someone tells the truth about their past and who they are. The truth is erotic. I have had clients who've asked: "What should I say about my past relationship?" I always suggest that they tell the truth. Even if you were an asshole, when you say it, you somehow become more attractive. One of my friends was living with a man who vowed that he had no secret agendas in his life, and she almost believed him until she found a marriage license when she was helping him put away his clothes.

Ending the Relationship

Dismissal is the only way that men leave a relationship, and it's important for all women who think they have no power, to understand this:

- Women do the choosing

- Women also do the ending

- Men disappear but only after they have been dismissed

- A woman will only dismiss a man after he has severely disappointed her.

So many women want to argue this point, but I still stick to my belief about this. A man in a relationship will only leave that woman if she sends him away. This may not be a dismissive action. Apathy, boredom, and silent disapproval, even on an unconscious level, can be construed as dismissal.

If you recall in Chapter 1, I mentioned meanness. For many women, meanness is an act of love. The fact that a woman has chosen this man to receive her anger indicates that she loves him and she trusts that he loves her and will not leave her. Women always have the choice to increase or temper their meanness if their man leaves clues that he is about to make an exit and she really doesn't want that. This is actually one of a woman's favorite ways to dismiss a man and still maintain that she is a victim of abandonment. Some women never get mean and bitchy; they are always sweet and compliant. These women are exceptionally dangerous. They will take out their anger in a passive-aggressive manner. Trust me about this; all women have anger at men.

Defining Your Boundaries for Intimacy

Kissing is the first decision that a woman must make when evaluating the expectations of dating. Just exactly how much intimacy is allowed? The woman gets to decide, of course. Men do not have the freedom to decide about a woman's body. Will you even allow him to touch your breast?

Many men think sex is included as a payback for the cost of the date. There is no discussion, the woman decides. When and where specifically the line gets drawn is a solo decision. If a man is too persistent before you are ready, he doesn't deserve to have you in his life.

My rule of thumb for clients is no sex for three months minimum. This is a point that stimulates much discussion. Men always think that three months is too long. Women must learn that they get to decide and if a man won't wait, he doesn't deserve to have her. That however, doesn't mean no touching. Handholding is fine, even on the first date but you get to decide where the end of your hand is. Frequently adults are stuck in the time warp of adolescence. The expectations of adult dating are much different and are affected by how long it has been since you went on your last date.

First dates are never the right time to have sex. In my opinion, it should be at least three months of steady interaction before anyone engages in sexual intimacy. My reason for saying this is that you can never go back to knowing who this person is before you had sex, if you've already done it.

Some people believe that sex is only acceptable after marriage. I am more liberal than that. If you don't know a person for who they really are and what kind of integrity they have, it is going to be very difficult to find that out once you have had sex. Somehow, everything changes. People do not behave the same towards each other after they have been sexually intimate.

Something about getting naked together interferes with the ability to talk. If a man doesn't want to date you because you won't have sex with him, he doesn't deserve to have you in his life. Sharing your body with someone is a sacred gift.

Beginning the Dating Process

Beginning the dating process in hopes of finding your ideal man and having a relationship is a big decision arising from a difficult mind-set because you always wonder where or how you'll ever meet him. Dating services facilitate the interaction of men and women by providing multiple profiles and choices defined by any number of criterion. On-line, computerized matching services and personal ads provide a plethora of opportunities for singles of all ages.

Avoiding intimacy can be achieved by just dating a lot of people or you can use that opportunity to make a lot of friends and learn how to relate to other adults in the dating realm. Becoming involved with someone is nothing more than testing each other to see if you meet the criteria which each of you defined in that description of your ideal person..

I recommend to my clients that they practice on as many people of the opposite sex as they can encounter. Women can test the men to see if they will produce for them and men can test the women to see if they learned how to effectively ask for and get what they want. They can test each other to see if there is compatibility through emotional, psychological, temperamental, or sexual attitudes.

Meeting someone who has been computer matched to you is no guarantee that they will be matched in more important ways such as chemistry, sexuality, and personality. Thus, the more people you meet, the more you will expand your comfort zone, and the more clarity you will get on what kind of person you actually want to choose. By meeting 40 new men, you are more likely to find someone who is compatible with you and wants to be with only you.

The Challenge: Meet Forty New Men and Test the Strategy

I recommend meeting forty new men, not necessarily dating, but meeting and having a meaningful conversation, to help you decide whether or not you like this person and why. Then you can decide if you want to see him again. Most important is whether you like this person, can get a feel for his human values, and can communicate with him.

In the beginning, do not worry about whether he likes you, is attracted to you, or wants to seduce you, other than for feedback. This is an experiment in stretching your comfort zone. You are not looking for a mate. You are learning about your own personal preferences. You are exploring your taste in men. This is an exercise and they are practice. Your focus must be on clarifying your preferences and learning how to ask for what you want. During the course of this exercise, more will be revealed to you about yourself, and the type of men that you have been attracted to in the past.

I have had clients tell me that this experience of meeting a lot of men has done amazing things for them. It opens up a part of them that they did not know existed. In the beginning, almost everyone hates it. At some point, they start to enjoy the experience. Later, they develop a sixth sense for knowing whether a man has the potential to be "it," and the final benefit is that the quality of men that they attract improves with each man they meet. This occurs because their self-esteem is constantly being nurtured.

Exclusivity Doesn't Mean Possession

Progression within a dating relationship nearly always indicates monogamous behavior. However, exclusivity doesn't mean possession. Exclusivity should mean that you have practiced on enough people that you can tell the difference between someone who is dating you because they want to get laid, and someone who is interested in having a serious relationship. I believe that honesty is the best idea in this case.

Asking for What You Want

If you want to get married, say so, even on the first date. That may scare away a few people but anyone who is interested in the same thing will stick around. You must be willing to risk losing everything you think you have, in order to get what you want.

If you are on a first date, you aren't risking much, and it's better to know that this person has no intentions other than to play if you are looking for a serious relationship. As adults, there are no solid reasons for playing teenage games. Why not say it like it is? I think a grown-up relationship is so much more attractive than carrying on an internal dialogue that sounds like this: "I wonder what he thinks of me?"

Scenario: Risking Everything for the Ideal Relationship

Kevin, age 57, met Caroline, age 55, in the Virgin Islands when they were introduced by mutual friends. They went out twice and both felt the chemistry between them. He lived in Washington State. She lived in the Virgin Islands. She was dating someone when they met but they were not in a committed relationship. He was not dating anyone at the time and after returning home, Kevin pursued Caroline through phone calls, e-mails, sending romantic cards and poetry. They stayed in touch for about a year, but didn't see each other during that time.

Eventually Kevin started dating a woman 20 years younger who lived near him, but he continued to call Caroline and indicated that he would like to come visit her. They talked about it, and both were encouraged because Caroline was planning to move to Dallas, Texas for business reasons. Let's listen in on the rest of their telephone conversation.

Kevin

I'll be in Dallas for a business seminar in December and would like to take you to dinner.

Caroline

That's five months from now. What happened with that woman you were dating?

Kevin

I've only been seeing Debbie for about a year now, but we have no plans for the future. I realize that we have an age discrepancy but we've gone to counseling and she's agreed that if the relationship continues that she'll honor my wishes of not having any children. You know, because my sons are already grown.

Caroline

Kevin, what are you doing? You have no plans for the future with her, but you're in counseling?

Kevin

She also has a few self-esteem issues. Whenever I make plans with other lady friends, like to play golf or have lunch, she is threatened. But you know me. They're just women friends, nothing more than that. At my age, I'm not going to change and she knows that. So, what do you say about dinner when I'm in town?

Caroline

We can talk about dinner in December, Kevin. In five months, a lot of things could be different. I have to run. Good-bye. (Caroline did not accept his invitation and she was direct in asking about the woman he was dating.) One month later, Kevin calls Caroline at her new home.

Kevin

I wanted to talk to you and give you my 800 number so we can stay in touch.

Caroline

Why? (Caroline is asking for his intentions in contacting her.)

Kevin

We had such a good time together on those first two dates and I'd like to see you again. Would you like to play golf, have dinner, or go swimming while I'm there? Oh, before you answer, I'd like your opinion on something. I'm going to be playing golf with a woman friend of mine tomorrow. My fiancé doesn't understand because she still has those self-esteem problems and doesn't trust me. Do you think, if you and I were in a committed relationship that it would be okay if I kept my female acquaintances, as long as it's only platonic?

Caroline

Hold it! Did you say fiancé? (Caroline did not buy into the conversation about dating or what he should do with his other women friends. She confronts him about having a fiancé. This skill is the ability to listen and recognize credibility gaps during a conversation.)

Kevin

I guess I haven't told you. We're engaged. I told her we could get married in four or five years. She wants to get married this September. So (chuckle) I might be married by the time I come to visit you. You wouldn't have a problem with that would you? (Kevin was trying to make a date five months in advance. This is a flaming red flag, especially since he knew already that he was engaged to another woman.)

Caroline

You are a very intelligent and attractive man and I enjoy our connection (acknowledgement). However, I don't want to see you after you are married. I want you to come here now (giving the order). If there is any possibility of a relationship between us, it would be better for you, me and your fiancé to find out now rather than later.

Kevin

I can't do that. We did have a connection and I could have expressed my "coulda, woulda, shoulda" desires to be with you, but that was then and this is now. When I asked you out to dinner, I was not thinking of you in that way.

Caroline

I'm not interested in being just another one of your women friends, so good bye, Kevin. Have a nice life and a happy marriage.

Scenario Analysis

Caroline took a risk in asking him to come and visit now. She was testing his commitment to the woman he was engaged to and looking for validation that he would produce results for her. She did not settle for a hope that there could be some sort of relationship in their future and she did not buy into discussing his perceptions about how relationships should be. She dismissed him because he showed a lack of integrity in the way he treats all women. In addition, it was obvious to Caroline that Kevin did not deserve to have her. He didn't deserve to have the woman he was engaged to either, but that really wasn't any business of Caroline's.

The "How to Get What You Want from Your Man Anytime" Strategy

- Be direct.

- Acknowledge him graciously and honestly.

- Use your appetite to ask for EXACTLY what you want.

- Ignore his hesitation and objections.

- Recognize when he violates one of your MAJOR standards and never settle.

- When he produces the result you want, show your appreciation.

- Dismiss him completely when he doesn't produce for you.

Chapter 3

Marriage Should be Like a Driver's License— Renewable Before It Expires

"Having a magical relationship won't happen just because you are in love. You have to work to make the magic keep happening."
—Barbara De Angelis, *Make Love Last a Lifetime*

Marriage is a state of togetherness based on the desire to trust another human being with your emotions, love, and innermost feelings. Is it really possible to have the kind of bond where you are together because you want to be together; and the thought would never cross your mind to violate that trust because this person means so much to you that you would die before you cheated on him? I believe that this is possible. I believe that you can build that kind of trust and vulnerability and that sacred trust is the foundation for all that happens in our lives.

I believe that a marriage can be the one sacred relationship in our lives that supports our dreams, inspires our achievements, and validates our integrity on a daily basis. I believe that it can be the foundation for a joyful life. Is this a fantasy? I don't think so. Is it the way of marriage in our country today? Not in the slightest. So what is the problem and what's missing?

When love is present, commitment happens. It's only children and financial obligations that create the necessity to make it legal. What could possibly cause such rampant deterioration of something that could be so beautiful? Perhaps marrying for the wrong reasons, or getting overwhelmed and lost in the day-to-day problems is what destroys marriages.

A lot of people thrive on vagueness. It seems to make life more acceptable for them. I think they strive for mediocrity. One of the purposes of an enlightened relationship is to solve problems and deal with past hurts. When you choose someone with whom you want to share your life, you are choosing to be vulnerable. Trusting that person will explore the painful injuries of past relationships and help you heal them.

Purchasing a house with someone requires a commitment. How the bills are divided and whose children live with you can define the relationship. Living together can be a roommate relationship situation or it can be a romantic relationship situation. The problems are similar and demand that you define your ground rules and boundaries before you set foot into any joint-dwelling arrangement. When your partner begins talking about the two of you living together, ask him: "What are your intentions for living with me?"

I had one client who moved in with a woman. She thought she was in a relationship and he thought he had a roommate. They lived together for several years in this arrangement. When he died, she was quite upset when she learned his point of view from his children.

Do You Really Need a Marriage License?

My personal opinion is that it isn't necessary to have a marriage license to have the kind of spiritual bond between a man and a woman that lasts a lifetime. In many cases, I think that the piece of paper actually causes the demise of the relationship. Once that license is issued and the vows are said, it seems that both the man and the woman start to take each other and the arrangement for granted. The affection, the sex, and the consideration that was shown to each other before the piece of paper, are now always there, so who has to pay attention?

It seems to me that the desire to be bonded is greatest before the bonding occurs. Once the bonding occurs, it feels more like chains holding you to a promise that you are not sure you want to keep. Why do we actually make the commitment of marriage? Is it for love or because it's expected?

Prenuptial agreements simply validate that marriage is a business agreement. A legal document created with the concept that this marriage will not last and this is what will happen if it doesn't last. In many ways a marriage is a small business. The property, house, cars, and furniture are the assets;

the children are the legacy; the income is the working capital; and love just doesn't quite fit in the business plan.

Any marriage can be a business agreement; our fantasies are that it is more than that. Little girls and boys believe in fairy tales and assume that their goal of living happily-ever-after is almost achieved when the wedding occurs. How true is this? The happily-ever-after part is only beginning at the time of the wedding. That is truly when all the work begins.

What Happened to the Magic of Togetherness?

How does one keep the specialness of love and the magic of togetherness fresh when the house is dirty? Life gets in the way of the fairy tale. Both of you are working different hours and the paychecks never seem to be enough. Marriage then becomes a legal agreement binding both parties to togetherness that isn't always magical. It's a lot of work.

Fear of being left behind is a reason for getting married. Age is a factor, and so is desperation. These are all factors that contribute to marriages that occur for the wrong reason. Instead of desiring to have that magical bond with the one person who you have tested and found to be your soul mate, people settle for who shows up.

We are a universe of scarcity. Arising from the point of view that there are not enough people to go around so that everyone can have a soul mate, women settle for men who don't produce for them, for men who are less than what they have described.

Men get married because it seems like the thing to do. They marry the most beautiful or the sexiest woman, thinking they can have all the sex they want, never even considering that this person might not have the same values or goals or even interests.

Who teaches us how to choose a mate? Who teaches us how and who to love? Our parents have the leading edge on the family and child relations course. Who taught them? Their parents as well, but things have changed. Men no longer have to be the sole provider, the macho hero, or the conqueror. Women no longer choose or wish to be the stay-at home subservient, obedient wife and mother.

Dead would be the time when we stop being attracted to the opposite sex. Possibly on a honeymoon, one would not notice someone physically attractive, but being married is not enough to stop being attracted to the opposite sex. In reality, attraction and chemistry can provide a catalyst for even greater sexual attraction between spouses. Two people cannot be everything to each other and in fact in those marriages where the couple excludes everyone from their life except each other, boredom sets in and the relationship deteriorates faster than ever.

Avoiding Marital Resentment

It is important to continue to grow and expand the person that you were when you first met each other. Inevitably, people who stop growing and stifle each other's creativity become resistant to each other, and start to resent that this is the only person in their life. Eventually, both the man and the woman will resort to revenge to free themselves from the monotony of monogamy.

Fear of being judged about sexuality, as well as ignorance about sexual freedom can create severe problems in a marriage. The culture and mores surrounding sexuality in this country is puritan. We are like someone floating on a raft in the ocean, surrounded by water but not a drop to drink. We are surrounded by sexuality, advertising, movies, music videos, and fashion and yet the amount of sexual freedom that exists in this country is miniscule.

Women lie to men about their sexual desires and their ability to feel pleasure. They are afraid to let a man know that they like sex because they fear being judged a slut. Yet, men indicate that they want a sexual woman, until they actually marry one. Then they want that sexuality suppressed just in case someone else might notice it.

What Happened to All the Sex?

In some marriages, women become property of their men. So what happened to all the sex that everyone thought they were going to get before marriage? It got lost in the translation. The result is that women are confused about their sexuality. While it is flaunted everywhere commercially, a woman who expresses her sexuality is considered a slut and is judged and ostracized by her peers, especially in the workplace.

At home, a woman cannot appear too experienced, for fear her new husband might think she previously slept around. Women have serious anxiety about their bodies and I believe it's unusual for any woman especially a new bride to feel uninhibited enough to tell a man how to touch her in a way that she can experience complete sexual satisfaction. So what occurs sexually is primarily left up to the creativity of the man and unless someone, a woman, has taught him how to satisfy a woman, there is most likely a serious gap in what that man knows and what he thinks he knows about sex.

Exhaustion is the primary reason for limited sexual encounters for young parents. Late hours, conflicts in schedules and simply an over-demanding life get in the way of sensual, romantic late-night seductions. Children are a great joy and one of the rewards of marriage if you want them. However, children are the most significant detractor from marriage and sex. The bad news about children is once you have them, you have them for life.

I am a grandmother and still my children interfere in my romantic adventures. They drop in, ask for babysitting services, and pass judgment on every man who I entertain. As a senior citizen woman seeking romance and a love interest, I can vouch for the fact that children are a significant obstacle to dating, love, and long-term relationships.

Scarcity Thinking

Scarcity thinking abounds in this country. Expectations about money and how it is handled reflect the patterns surrounding finance that each person experienced in their own family. Merging two individual strategies about money can create violent and radical disagreements between spouses. Why is money such a volatile topic in marriage? It's likely because it is so personal and so necessary and because most people come from scarcity. So few people agree on how money should be handled in a family. Some people are savers, some are spenders, some are cautious, some are careless, and some don't even consider money an issue.

For example, my former husband thought as long as he had an ATM card and that money would come out of the machine, he had money to spend. He never gave a second thought to whether the money in the bank had already been spent. The merging of two financial backgrounds to evolve into a married couple's strategy for financial freedom is a great challenge, and based on the amount of credit card debt and bankruptcies in this country, I would say it is another area of life that has been sorely neglected in the upbringing of humans.

What Killed the Marriage?

Schedules, work hours, children, extended family, shared childcare, and household duties all contribute to the life "overwhelm" which interferes with people being in love. Before marriage, time is devoted to the relationship exclusively. After marriage, with or without children, the business of life interferes with relating. Unless specific time is dedicated to the care and nurturing of a relationship, it's guaranteed that loving time will be relegated to a lower priority. Life just interferes.

When a romance is new, everything else can wait. Once the commitment has been made, men go into production mode and are about creating reserves of money, security and support for their families. Women slip into nesting, creating a home, nurturing children and though all of these things are essential to family life, love goes on the back burner until someone notices the flame has gone out. To add to all this, most parents who work are too tired to be in love.

Security and Comfort Issues

Security is a reason that people who have been married for twenty years sell out. The comfort and money that have been accumulated by those married couples who have managed to stay together through the early years of marriage and raising children create a trap for themselves when they have settled for security in place of love.

I know too many couples in their fifties with grown children who won't consider a divorce but who are absolutely miserable together. They have sold themselves down the river for security and comfort. They have long ago given up on passion, sensuality, sex, and love. They are just comfortable and are willing to settle for that. Some don't even talk to each other; they simply live separate lives from under the same roof.

I believe this is especially true of families who have a lot of children, where the mother raised the children alone while the father worked long hard hours to create the money to support his big family. When the children leave, what is left is the shell of a marriage and two people who don't even know each other anymore. There are those who attempt to reacquaint themselves with each other, but many do not. They just settle for mediocrity in their relationship. I am not willing to have a mediocre relationship under any circumstances.

Scenario: Comfort and Security Issues

Dorie and George had been married for twenty-seven years. He was a successful business man, and she was a housewife with seven children and three more adopted children. All she had ever wanted to do was to be a mother and housewife, and so she had achieved her lifetime objective.

George, however, wanted to participate in politics and social events and they constantly argued over her lack of participation. George would go alone and as was inevitable, he became involved with other women. The other women would come and go and Dorie would just ignore them, knowing that her husband and the father of her children would never leave her. She rationalized in her mind that these were just women for his amusement.

By the time that Dorie came to me, her youngest child was 16 and in high school. She was quite unhappy with her marital situation. She felt afraid of being left home alone all of the time. The children had all left and gone on with their own lives. She wanted more attention from George and had the following conversation with him.

Dorie

George, you have always been a great provider and father to the children. You are so successful in your business and I have always been proud of your achievements. You have been a wonderful husband to me, too. I want you to start including me in your life more. I know that I have always resisted the social situations, but now that the children are grown, I have more time to be involved in your social affairs.

George

What do you really want, Dorie?

Dorie

I want to know that you still love me.

George

I've always loved you and you know it. So what is it you really want?

Dorie

Pay more attention to me. You never talk to me anymore and you hardly ever touch me.

George

You never wanted to be touched. After Cindy (the 16 year old) you didn't seem to be much interested in sex.

Dorie

I didn't want to have another child but now there is no fear of that. I am too old.

George

So you want me to turn it back on again. I'm not sure I can.

Dorie

I want you to try.

Six months passed and nothing changed. George still ignored Dorie, and they were still sleeping in separate beds.

Scenario Analysis

Dorie wasn't willing to take any risks with her marriage. She told me that she couldn't give up the security of her home and her status as George's wife and the support that the children in college received, and she just couldn't tolerate the stigma of being a divorced woman. She settled for staying in her marriage and George continued to party and see other women.

Innocent Encounters

Innocent encounters often lead to not so innocent flirting. There is a line to cross with flirting that will provide visible evidence of relationship deterioration. Everyone flirts. Married, unmarried, engaged; it doesn't matter. Flirting is a pastime and it makes life interesting. In many cases, it is a good thing, causing stimulation of serotonin in married people's brains, which cause them to go home and be seductive with their spouse. There is nothing more fun than an innocent workplace flirtation, as long as it remains innocent.

Young teens learn how to flirt and the custom continues throughout everyone's life. The encounter of an older woman with a charming young box boy at the grocery store can make her day, possibly his too if he is willing to learn from the exposure. A mature man winks at a cute receptionist in order to gain access to her boss. So what is the problem? There isn't one as long as flirting continues to be just that. It is when flirting crosses that line into seduction and serious violation of intimacy between strangers that flirting becomes a problem.

Negotiating Your Boundaries

Boredom is a big culprit in the area of cheating. A little flirting is followed by some dishonesty, and then guilt and then exposure, and finally revenge.

From my perspective, there are only rare exceptions to the fact that adultery, cheating, or affairs are *symptoms* of long-standing marital problems. Everyone who gets married expects adherence to the same standards as far as fidelity is concerned. However, the romantic assumption is that everyone gets married because they are passionately in love and that fidelity is the highest value of marriage.

Here is a couple who thinks that they are in love. One of them lies about something or breaks a promise, or does something that totally violates the other's ethics, but they are in love and s/he is so perfect otherwise. It's just a small thing, and certainly a little thing like that is tolerable. After all, they are getting married and that means they can work it out. Love conquers all.

Here is the problem. Love doesn't solve anything. People come to agreement or negotiate boundaries and decide to be together because they want to be together. They choose marriage. I think the rules of marriage and the boundaries that each couple wants to live by must be negotiated. Obviously, each scenario cannot be discussed ahead of time, but the individual standards of each partner in each marriage must be decided prior to the vows. When a woman or man settles (that includes compromises, tolerates, or sells out) on a value that is significant to his or her partner, the bond is compromised. It makes it okay to do it again, whatever "it" is.

Applying the Strategy

According to my strategy, women have the power in relationship and their job is to provide appetite, which challenges the man who loves her to produce results. The man who wants to please his woman will produce those results as long as she believes in him and respects him as the producer.

The other component in this neat little package is the sex. Men will do anything for sex. Women love sex as much as men do; it's just not socially acceptable for them to say so. Men get their pleasure from a woman's pleasure and "most women lie to men about their satisfaction" which leads to a giant gap in the presumption that marriage defines passionate, romantic love and fidelity as the highest values.

It means life gets in the way of relationship and unless some time and energy is devoted to the relationship as an entity, that state of "in love" that everyone marries into will disintegrate. There are exceptions, but men and women, at the time of their marriage, do not intend to be unfaithful, nor do they seek out an affair.

Here is how an affair begins:

1. One or the other partner is not getting his/her needs met for whatever reasons.

2. That person encounters someone at work, or at a party, or in the neighborhood, who notices him or her and sees something that attracts. (There is nothing like a flirtation to restore a sense of self-esteem.)

3. Initially, the married person resists, but enjoys the attention.

4. The spouse that's been out goes home to the other spouse and hints that he or she needs more attention.

5. The spouse at home makes two assumptions: a) they are married so there is nothing to worry about; and, b) there will be plenty of time to take care of their spouse's needs later. Because that spouse is involved in the drama of daily life; the hint is ignored.

That, my friends, is the beginning of the affair. When one partner seeks intimate, emotional, physical, or intellectual support from someone of the opposite sex outside of the marriage, the seed has been sown. There are no innocent victims among the three people involved in an extramarital affair. Everyone plays a part.

It seems that marriage is frequently taken for granted. The almighty wedding ring is supposed to be able to bind people to their vows automatically. This, I believe, is the false presumption that leads us to the incorrigible statistic that 80% of marriages are affected by infidelity.

Marriage doesn't work by itself. It takes two people who pay attention to each other's needs. It takes two people who believe in each other and validate each other. It takes two people who want to love each other and who continually approve of each other which allow the vulnerability necessary to be honest about their personal needs.

Vulnerability and connection are two of the elements necessary to keep a marriage from becoming just another obligation. It is necessary for both people in a relationship to grow, I agree. However, I believe it is more important for them to remain totally honest with each other and to consistently be vulnerable with each other, sharing disappointments, mistakes, failures, bad judgment, and joy. Without that vulnerability, each of them becomes separate. They are no longer bound together in a marriage. They are simply two individuals sharing the same roof dealing with their challenges in life individually. From that point on, the relationship will suffer. Once that intimate bond has been severed, it is difficult to reconnect. Each goes on believing that the other is content, handling life and doesn't need to share their joys and disappointments. It is then that marriage becomes an obligation.

Love strained by separate paths leads to the too simple solution of divorce. Undelivered "withholds" create a barrier between lovers. Children are sometimes the only things holding a couple together. Divorce is the easy way out. It has become one of the earlier avenues to take rather than honoring the commitment of marriage vows. I don't mean to be pious here, but divorce is not the only solution when communication has been severed. What about reconnecting and creating some honesty between the spouses?

I agree that relationships can deteriorate rapidly; however, I also believe that it wouldn't be impossible to reconnect a lot of people who take divorce as the easy way out. The release of hurt feelings, abandonment of rigid beliefs, the willingness to be vulnerable and the belief that this person that you once loved will not violate your trust are the ingredients necessary to mend a fractured relationship.

My personal goal for this work is to decrease the divorce rate in this country by 10% in the next ten years.

Keeping Your Marriage Alive

Renewable vows, separate living situations, and dedication to the belief in togetherness are a few ways that might keep a marriage fresh. What if marriage licenses were renewable? Wouldn't that call for those who were married to be forced to evaluate their marital situation regularly?

I am not a believer in governmental interference, but I just think that by choice people could choose to reevaluate their life, their goals, their principals, and their values to see if they remain on the same path. An evaluation like that could prevent some of the wandering separate ways that occurs in many marriages.

Personally, I believe that once marriage vows have been taken, many married couples think that is the end of their need to communicate about shared values and goals. It seems to me that wedding rings are like prison doors—once you are inside you can forget about having to take care of personal needs, and it becomes automatic. To keep your marriage alive, you must pay attention to each other's needs, and be dedicated to your commitment to each other.

The "How to Get What You Want from Your Man Anytime" Strategy

- Be direct.

- Acknowledge him graciously and honestly.

- Use your appetite to ask for EXACTLY what you want.

- Ignore his hesitation and objections.

- Recognize when he violates one of your MAJOR standards and never settle.

- When he produces the result you want, show your appreciation.

- Dismiss him completely when he doesn't produce for you.

Chapter 4

Who Has the Power?

"The feeling that men are more susceptible to seduction can be countered by the fact that women get swept up in romance, and in the end, in love, we are all vulnerable, and women should not be seen as dangerous because we are desirable."

—Elizabeth Wurtzel, *Bitch*

Creativity, circular thinking, and intuition are just a few of the characteristics which allow women to enjoy the journey of life rather than the destination. The female sex has the power in relationship. From the time of their birth, women are into relating and communicating. The entire male sex rarely encompasses the art of relating unless a woman shows them the way. It is a gift that a woman brings to a man.

I want to take a slight diversion here in order to make something perfectly clear. Men are not the bad guys. I love men. They are these wonderfully creative, industrious, productive, sensitive, charming creatures who love to build things, solve problems, satisfy their physical needs, (i.e. belch, fart, eat, sleep, climax, and play with gadgets), as well as please the women they love. What they are not interested in doing is engaging in talk about their relationship, guessing what their woman wants, shopping, or being judged, disapproved of or nagged. They love sex. They love doing it, thinking about it, talking about it, reading about it and they believe that sex is affection.

Yes, I believe that men are sensitive, extremely so, to be exact. I think they get their feelings hurt perhaps easier than women do. The difference is they don't show it. They don't cry or even get angry, they just stuff it inside and withdraw to lick their wounds until they scar over and they are ready to go back out and fight the good fight again. I believe that men feel slighted when one of their projects is taken for granted. They feel hurt and doubt their production when they are looked over for promotion. I believe that a woman can devastate them with a look, or an innocent comment like "You did what?" or if she doesn't notice or approve or appreciate his efforts on her behalf. I believe that men are always trying to please women and their biggest dilemma is that they don't have a clue how to accomplish this because women think differently than men.

I believe that men appreciate women who tell them what they want them to do. I believe that men cherish women who are honest with them and who don't play games. I believe that men are attracted to women who have appetites for pleasure and women who demonstrate their pleasure both verbally and physically. I believe that men think when they are rejected by a woman that the woman doubts their production (money, success, sex as in erections) in some way. I believe that a man does not inherently know how to physically please a woman, and that each woman is different, therefore, each woman must teach her man. Finally, I believe that men will do just about anything for sex.

A while ago, I witnessed one of the toughest, macho, ex-marine construction foremen I know do a beautiful thing. When one of the women in our office got married, this man made a point to find out her favorite color and the size of their bed, and ordered some very fine monogrammed linens for her. He arrived at her office with a large cardboard box. He put it on her chair and told her gruffly that someone delivered the box to his office by mistake. After she opened the box, he made a few slightly suggestive jokes about what she and her new husband were going to do on their new sheets. She was very touched and tried to thank him but he just turned bright red and sloughed off the appreciation. It was obvious to me that this macho man has a very tender, romantic side to him that he is embarrassed to reveal, but still will because he has the honor and integrity of a man. I believe that men are like this all the time.

Before my mother died, she was in a nursing home with Alzheimer's. My dad who was a contractor and president of every organization he ever joined, is the epitome of macho. He visited my mother daily. After a while, she did not even recognize him and could not carry on a conversation. He'd turn off his hearing aid and just talk to her about what was going on in his life and with all of their 6 children. Then he would paint her finger nails, curl and brush her hair and take her for ice-cream. This went on for several years until she died. I would never have imagined that my dad could have been so tender and caring, but he was.

I was present at the birth of my first grandchild along with my son-in-law. I watched as my daughter delivered her son and the doctor checked him and then handed him to my son-in-law. Jason was so moved by the birth of his son that as he held him in his hands, tears rolled down his face. I have seen this scene repeated again and again at the many births I have witnessed.

At my husband's funeral, there were about a thousand men, visibly shaken, some so shook up they could not speak, but those who did spoke of his commitment to them as men and how he had sacrificed to teach them to change their lives from pre-delinquent to upstanding citizen, mayor, school principal, police officer, business owner, fathers and coaches. He accomplished this as a man, actually as a wrestling coach who took the toughest boys he could find on the street and taught them to channel their aggression into an acceptable form where they could become champions and experience success.

What do all of these examples prove? They prove that men are our heroes, saviors, gladiators, and rescuers. They represent honor, integrity, and toughness. They fight for what they believe, and they are the first to come to the rescue of a damsel, child, or animal in distress. They perform these tasks silently, not asking for praise or recognition. They are stoic, often working while sick or in pain, frequently refusing to see a doctor until they are severely ill. They come across as tough guys and are unwilling to show their emotions for fear of being thought a wimp. It is these traits that make them our heroes and yet frequently they are characterized as unemotional, detached, and macho.

Our American society puts a lot of pressure on men to perform, control their emotions, be tough, and live within a tight definition of what is masculine. Then we criticize them for being the way that we have pressured them to be.

Personally I love men just the way they are. More sex is always better and, being catered to and rescued by a man makes me feel petite, feminine, and safe. As far as I am concerned macho is sexy, Don Johnson and Mel Gibson still give me palpitations.

I'm aware that the generalizations in this book favor women, but the scales have been tipped the other direction for a long time and this book is directed mainly at women so it's going to be a little unbalanced.

Jack Rafferty, who taught several of the Man/Woman courses I attended, said that men are dumb about women and almost all of them will admit that. He also said that men are simple creatures with few requirements for comfort. Most can get by with a refrigerator, a bed and a remote control for the TV and that is why a woman will always enhance the quality of life for a man.

Women bring fullness to life, passion into relationships, and intimacy into sex. For men, sex is an act, devoid of emotion. It's about pure physical pleasure only. It takes a woman to lead a man into full sexual surrender and the experience of passion and intimacy that is available only to those who are willing to risk losing everything they have in order to get what they want. A man who surrenders to a woman's power in relationship will reap rewards he doesn't even know exist.

Orders given by a woman are not about control. They are simply very clear requests. A woman being a bitch doesn't mean that she is evil, vindictive, nasty or mean. Bitch by my definition means that she knows what she wants and asks for it in a way that any man, woman, or child can understand what she is requesting and always expects to receive it if not from the man in front of her then from someone else. Note: There are evil, vicious bitches who are mainly interested in revenge. They have been hurt by someone. This book has been written to try to prevent any of you from becoming this kind of bitch.

The type of a bitch that I would like all of my clients to become is a woman who can approve of a man, ask directly for what she wants, and then show overwhelming appreciation in a way that a man can understand. Power in a relationship is not about control. It is about surrender. Those of you who are evolved enough to get this can appreciate that total surrender to another human being does not give them power over you. It simply gives power and strength to the relationship. It is that ability to be vulnerable with another human being that begets surrender and achieves the level of integrity and commitment that is necessary for a truly passionate love relationship.

Power is about Trust and Surrender

Trust in one another is essential for surrender to occur. Both the man and the woman surrender to each other in relationship not just in terms of sexuality, but also in terms of life. The outcome of their relationship depends on whether a man can surrender to his woman steering the relationship and whether the woman can surrender to her man's physical strength and protection even though she doesn't really need it.

Surrender means vulnerability. It means trusting that this person to whom you have committed will be there when you need him. It means that each of you can be wrong, make mistakes, do stupid things, be intentionally dumb, and even violate your own standards against yourself and in spite of all that, your partner will stand by you and believe in you while you work your way out of the dilemma that you have created. It means that there is a bond which cannot be broken; that no matter what, your love will persist. Mutual surrender means that this relationship comes first before anything else, and that includes people, jobs, money, and family. No matter what, the relationship is the foundation for your life. You, as a couple, are always on the same side.

The reality is that men have the power. They are bigger, stronger, and hold higher positions in business and politics. They are macho, controlling, and get general acknowledgement from everyone who matters that they have the power. In this world, everyone matters.

Is it not true that men live in the fantasy that they have all the power in the world? Yes it is so, but if we look deeper, we will find that behind every great man there is usually a great woman who believes in him. It is women who empower the men to produce the fantastic results that they are able to achieve. It is a woman's complaining that is the driving force for technological improvements that men create while they are trying to please the women.

On the surface, it appears true that men have more power than women, but underneath it all, women have the strength to ask for what they want. Women endure childbirth and pain, and the stress of raising children much easier than the physically, stronger male. Women do have power; feminine power.

Sacrificing their integrity by withholding the truth and lying to avoid confrontation are some of the ways that men behave as wimps. Men are not wimps in reality. Men will go to extremes to avoid hurting women. Many men believe they are protecting women by not telling them the truth. What they're forgetting is that honesty in relationship is the most powerful tool that exists in the world. Although their intention is honorable, the end result reveals that indeed their behavior is less than acceptable, because they did not tell the truth. They simply wanted to avoid confrontation. Sound confusing? It is, and imagine what it is like inside the mind of the man who is trying to manage all of this.

If a man's motivation is to take care of the women in his life, he will always act on what he believes is their highest good. The problem is that men have a defective interpretation of what women's standards of highest good are. It isn't protection from the truth. It is gut level honesty that will win a woman, and bring power and integrity to a relationship.

Nagging, mean, castrating bitches are what women are perceived to be in the conceptual image of a wife. Women are not vultures. Women only resort to nagging, bitchy behavior when men don't respond to their requests. Granted, most women don't know how to ask a man for something, so that he can hear the request, but that is what this book is all about.

When I speak of the spiral effect of positive relationships where both parties approve of each other, and ask for what they want, and appreciate what is offered by their partner, the reverse is also true. The spiral can work in reverse where a woman does not approve of her man and asks for what she wants, and because he knows she does not believe he will produce, he doesn't. This creates more disapproval and nagging, which is whining about what hasn't been done. Eventually what happens is men give up trying, and women turn into the other kind of mean, nasty, castrating bitch, and they both take revenge on each other.

Women get the nag label honestly, because they never learned the productive way of asking for what they want. They are taught to be coy, unselfish, and beautiful rather than being taught how to approve, ask, and receive graciously with over-the-top appreciation.

The Lonely Woman Syndrome

Loneliness is a side effect of a woman's independence. The rise in self-esteem that a woman gets by being able to take care of herself and in many cases her children as well, does not compensate for the emptiness that arises when she does not have a man in her life. Women are not amazons even though they are capable of incredible accomplishments. What women achieve by behaving as amazons is their independence from men. In spite of their ability to be independent in many ways, women still want and need men to love them and be with them in relationship.

Perhaps crashing through the glass ceiling or entrepreneurial success or simply the ability to support herself and her children after a divorce, is cause for celebration and recognition of her incredible power as a female human being. Unfortunately, having no one to share these accomplishments with accentuates the void, which cultivates that instinctive drive to have a partner by her side.

It is lonely being wonder woman and most women that I know would prefer not to do it alone. Most women love men. Most women love what men are about. What most women don't love is being controlled and subjugated by a man. What would happen if men and women could be partners in passion and love and life?

Notice who chooses whom in a relationship. There may be mutual attraction but who actually decides whether the relationship is a go or not? I say that it is the woman who does the choosing. The way I believe that it works is that a woman will notice a man and be attracted to who he is by his behavior. Although his physical appearance enters into the picture, anyone with real integrity about relationship knows that looks are superficial, and who this person is on a cellular, intuitive, intimate level is what attraction is really about.

If a man notices a woman first, and acknowledges that he wants to meet her, then he must get himself in front of her so that she can give him the go-ahead signal. She will only do this if he has produced some result which attracts her.

We all know that there are relationships that start purely from physical attraction, but that doesn't mean that they continue just because the physicality is there. There must be more substance to a relationship than just physical chemistry or the relationship cannot survive the intensity of life. All in all, both parties must prove themselves as a match in terms of values, integrity, desires, wants, needs, sexuality, and behaviors in order for a relationship to continue past the initial chemistry.

Disillusionment and Dismissal

Disillusionment is usually the point at which a relationship ends. Generally speaking, there must be a last straw which results in the dismissal of the man in the relationship. Yes, I am stating unequivocally that women end relationships as well as they do the choosing.

Many times it appears that a man will leave, and then the woman feels abandoned. However, a man will only leave a committed relationship when he has been dismissed. I am speaking about the long-term, solid marriages and long-term pre-engagement relationships when I talk about women ending the relationship.

Here's how it works. A man will do something to totally disillusion the woman. She will want to excuse it, but underneath her forgiveness will be that nagging feeling that if she forgives this issue, she will be settling for less than what she wants in a relationship. When a woman settles, both parties lose.

The man must rise to her standards in order for the relationship to succeed. I don't know why exactly women get to choose. I think it is because in truth, women are about appetite and about relating, whereas men are about production and end results.

The most difficult task for a woman to perform is to dismiss a man who is 99% what she wants and who only has one fatal flaw. But that flaw is the one item that can destroy a relationship. If she settles, I promise you that one flaw will be the ultimate destruction of the relationship, even if it's twenty-three years later.

Scenario: Discover Your Place in His Priorities

Karen and Gregg met through Craig's list, a California matching service that connects people with similar interests and hobbies. They were both very attracted to each other. The only negative that Karen uncovered about Gregg was that he liked smoking pot. It was an issue for her because her ex-husband had been addicted to marijuana, and it had seriously damaged their marriage. She couldn't tolerate being around it and she didn't like the smell of it.

Initially, she told Gregg how she felt about pot, and he said honestly that he didn't know if he could give it up, but that he would not smoke in front of her. He also promised her that he would tell her if he felt he needed to indulge. She accepted that, and they continued to see each other. Occasionally, Gregg would tell her that he had wanted to smoke pot but that he had refrained from doing it because he knew how she felt about it. Karen had now decided that he could be the man she would marry, and they progressed to having greater intimacy which included sex.

One weekend they went on a camping trip. During the trip, Gregg said he wanted to go off on a hike by himself to enjoy nature. Karen didn't mind and she stayed at the camp site and read. Gregg went for a hike for a couple of hours, and when he returned, he smelled of pot. Karen knew, both from his visual affect and the smell that he had smoked pot, but she waited for him to bring up the subject. He didn't.

The incident severely bothered Karen, and she discussed this with me. She wanted to know what to do. After talking about it more, Karen realized that this issue was a "do or die" for her concerning their relationship. She decided to discuss it one more time with Gregg.

Karen

Gregg, I have been so happy for the past six months, and it has been exciting and wonderful being with you. The sex is great. We have so much in common. I really love being around you. Last week when we were camping, I know that you smoked some pot. I could smell it on your clothes. It has been bothering me ever since because you didn't tell me and you apparently hid it from me.

Gregg

I didn't hide it. I just didn't think it was that big of a deal. I have always smoked when I was out in nature and it seemed very natural to me. Are you going to make an issue of it?

Karen

I spent a lot of time thinking about this. Because of my past experience with my former husband and how I feel about smoking pot and drug usage in general, I realized that this is a big deal to me. I can't stand the smell of it and it makes me so uncomfortable to know that you are doing it that I can't be with you if you smoke pot.

Gregg sits quietly for about 10 seconds, then stands, picks up his jacket and walks out of the room and out of the front door.

Scenario Analysis

Karen called me, very distraught and confused, as to how Gregg could have so easily discarded their love and the intimacy they had shared just to smoke pot. He wasn't the man she thought he was. She wasn't willing to settle for him being less than what she wanted in a mate. This is an important point. Karen didn't necessarily have the right to demand that Gregg stop smoking pot. As an adult, that is his choice. However, she does have the right to decide if she will allow someone who smokes pot to be in her life or not. In this scenario, she was direct and stood up for what she wanted. She didn't settle.

Increasing Your Appetite within a Relationship

Clarity about what a woman wants is always a challenge for her. The fact that she is deserving of what she wants is not the issue. It is the need for constantly expanding appetite that becomes overwhelming for most women.

I have clients who have successfully mastered this strategy, who only call me for coaching when they recognize that they are running out of appetite. The conversation goes something like this:

"What do I do now? I have everything that I have ever wanted and I recognize that when I don't have appetite for my husband, he loses interest in producing for me. Then we start to have problems in our relationship."

The most difficult thing for each and every woman to achieve is the ability to continually increase her appetite and to be able to express it, because that's what it takes for the relationship to work. Women have been raised to be unselfish, and it feels selfish for some women to ask for more than what their husbands think they can produce.

It has been proven to me over and over that appetite is truly a woman's responsibility in the relationship. Men like to produce results. They love to win, score, and be successful. When women ask for things like more intimacy, more success, to start a business, to live their dream, have another child, go back to school, buy a new house, take a risk and change their life, it provides men the opportunity to do these things and get their own needs satisfied as well.

Challenging a Man Increases His Production

Challenge is the one thing that will cause a man to produce more than he thinks he can. A bottom line truth is that men want to please women. Another bottom line truth is that all men are macho and competitive. Therefore, when a man loves a woman and wants to please her, and she asks him for something that is more than he thinks he can produce, and she believes without a doubt that he can produce it, he will do it.

No man that I know will tell his woman that he is unable or cannot do what she asks. I suppose it appears that the woman is then playing on his macho tendencies to get what she wants, but what if we could look at it from the perspective of win-win? A woman with clarity asks her man to produce a result bigger than he believes he can. She believes in him so much that he rises to the occasion and produces that big result.

Therefore, they both win because she gets what she wants; he grows and becomes a bigger and more accomplished person; and therefore, his belief in himself increases and then the bigger challenges become accomplishments. The woman grows in self-esteem because she has expressed her appetite and has been rewarded for believing in him. The man grows in self-esteem because he succeeds at something he wasn't sure he could do. Then they celebrate while she approves of him and acknowledges his success. This is truly a win-win.

When anyone accomplishes a goal against overwhelming odds, the charge that accompanies it is an even greater victory than imagined. Therefore, when a woman believes in a man and by her belief alone, he accomplishes a challenge, the bond between them expands exponentially. This is part of the profound intimacy that develops in long-term relationships. When we talk about who has the power in relationship, it occurs to me that the power that women have with men is faith.

Unfortunately, women are accustomed to living as second class citizens who play traditional roles. It's difficult for me to describe in writing the stretch necessary for a woman to become the kind of woman that a man will produce for under any circumstances. The first woman who I ever met who embodied all of the traits that I speak of in this book was someone I met while attending my first Man-Woman Course from Jack Rafferty.

She was married to one of his neighbors and she had this unbelievable charisma about her. She could walk into any room, with any number of people in it, and immediately become the center of attention. Everyone, men and women alike, would put out tremendous effort to get her whatever she requested. She was immensely powerful, beautiful, gracious, and charming. It was immediately apparent to all of us women in the class that the gap that existed from where she lived and where we lived was enormous.

It takes an inordinate amount of self-esteem to know that you are loved by yourself enough to have whatever you want from whomever you want it and not let your ego run amok. This is the edge: being able to remain a most powerful woman who can honestly express her appetite constantly and still be gracious, charming and be loved and cherished by those around her.

Don't Settle For Less Than You What You Want in a Relationship

Settling for less than what you want in any situation is a critical point in every relationship. A woman must assume her power in the relationship or the relationship will suffer. The turning point in every relationship is when the woman recognizes that unless this man produces at the level to which she holds the bar, she will be settling and will give up her power.

Someone must steer the relationship and in a male-female relationship that must be the woman because she is the one who enhances the quality of life for everyone around her. A man does not care about taking the relationship anywhere. Men are not about relating. They are about producing.

Have you ever met a man who wanted to talk about, plan for, or discuss his relationship? A man will produce to the level of his woman's appetite and no more. That is the bottom line to how relationship works. I know I sound like a broken record and that it appears as if this is the only strategy that works in relationship. It's certainly not the only strategy, but it is one that works. Why settle for less than a woman can imagine?

Satisfaction, love, intimacy, passion, contentment, and achievement are possible when a man and woman empower their relationship with this strategy The woman will raise the bar on her standards, and when she doesn't know that her job in relationship is to produce appetite to drive the accomplishments, the committed relationship will flounder and eventually fail.

It's interesting to note that in Forbes magazine they listed the 200 richest people in the world. Only ten of those were women. Another fact to consider is that there were only about ten of those men who weren't married. All the rest were married and their wives were not necessarily business people. So if my theory is true, then all those women who are married to the richest men in the world certainly know how to express their appetite; at least when it comes to financial matters. If only all women could understand that it isn't just tangible challenges. Their appetites also work when asking for behavioral changes in their man as well. Over the years, I've listened to many of my clients say, "I just want my man to show up in the relationship. I want him to pay attention to me. I want him to make love to me all of the time."

Ladies, if you want it all, you must experiment with your appetite on the intangibles as well.

The "How to Get What You Want from Your Man Anytime" Strategy

- Be direct.

- Acknowledge him graciously and honestly.

- Use your appetite to ask for EXACTLY what you want.

- Ignore his hesitation and objections.

- Recognize when he violates one of your MAJOR standards and never settle.

- When he produces the result you want, show your appreciation.

- Dismiss him completely when he doesn't produce for you.

Chapter 5

Keeping the Magic Alive

"... There was just all this amazing light, very bright but not the least stark. In fact this light was soft-almost like a cloud. I remember feeling a sensation of not being physically there anymore, just floating in that bright, safe, peaceful light. I must have had an orgasm at that point, but this feeling was beyond orgasm. It was a feeling of spiritual connection so deep I can't even describe it. ... This is the way it's supposed to be. This is what they mean when they talk about seeing fireworks and hearing angels sing."

—Dr. Sandra Scantling and Sue Browder
Ordinary Women Extraordinary Sex

A promise backed by integrity and presented to the world by a declaration is a stand for love. It is also marriage, commitment and a sacred bond. Taking a stand for being in love so that nothing, no upset, mistake or turn of events can invalidate the declaration and commitment to each other's love, is the kind of relationship that is required in marriage.

Unfortunately, today that isn't usually the case. Marriage today is something like a promise that screams, "I will love you until you disappoint me, and then I will leave you and divorce you." The type of relationship for which I search and I believe that most people who really are ready for relationship seek is demonstrated by taking a stand for love. No one who is ready for love wants a temporary relationship.

I have witnessed people who have taken such a stand which resulted in their love, marriage, and relationships transcending any and all difficulties, challenges, and mistakes that they encountered. Marriage used to be the vehicle that provided that insurance. We have lost that ability to take a stand for love and this is what I seek and what the people, whom I coach, seek. Is it possible to have that kind of love? I believe it is, but it's a decision that you make at the time that you take a stand for love. Faithfulness and commitment is a conscious decision.

Awareness of your own personal needs and honest communication with your mate are necessary to support authenticity. The stand for love is what makes a relationship thrive.

To get your needs met by anyone, you must know yourself and what those needs are. Part of the reality that leads to the 50% divorce rate in this country is the almost universal ignorance of what it is that each of us wants. If we do not know what we want, we cannot communicate it to another person. Subsequently, that other person cannot produce fulfillment of those undefined needs.

So we all operate in vagueness, guessing about what each other wants and usually we guess wrong. What is the cost? Family dysfunction, divorce, pain, suffering, broken homes, traumatized children, and broken hearts are the cost.

Be Honest With Yourself

The first step toward a positive and loving relationship is being honest with yourself. Examine your personal needs and desires. Love who you are, and be ecstatic about the gift of being female. Once you begin to know who you are and what you want, you can then learn how to communicate it to someone who cares.

Trust is the primary ingredient in a stand for love. Jealousy and doubt can destroy love if it is allowed to fester. Nothing activates a woman's meanness like jealousy. Jealousy can be activated as quickly as flipping on a light switch. One moment it's off; the next, it's on. A woman will exhibit jealousy whenever it is triggered by something which threatens her self-image or her relationship. Like a mother protecting her cubs, a jealous woman will exhibit "meanness" to her man when she envisions that another woman is the cause of her insecurity.

She is willing to share her anger with him because she finally trusts that he will not leave her. Ironically, it is only her meanness that will finally drive a man to that desperate point of leaving the woman he loves.

A man will not leave a woman unless the woman has dismissed him and sent him packing. She will only share her basic anger with a man who she truly loves and trusts. So actually a woman's meanness is an act of love. Sound contradictory? It is. Men do not understand this about women because they do not know why women have to be mean. A woman's underlying reason for being mean is that she has always been treated like second-class citizen, dominated by men, and subjugated in relationship.

When a man's behavior triggers jealousy in a woman, she doubts her attractiveness, which threatens her self-esteem, which in turn escalates the underlying anger into full overt rage. Men only see the overt anger. Men are unaware that women have this underlying anger because they don't acknowledge that women are victims of discrimination. Men and women take for granted the way that women are treated by business people, waiters, auto mechanics, car salesmen, physicians, and anyone of authority.

Women are ignored, patronized, humored, and discounted in so many ways that it is impossible to describe them all. I know I sound like sour grapes here, but that is not my purpose. I want to raise the level of consciousness for whoever is reading this so that they may become more aware of when such slights occur, so that action can be taken by women to minimize these occurrences in the future.

Women are people, too. We do have rights as human beings. Many of us pay our own way and are responsible for not only ourselves but children or parents as well. It isn't only men who pay their way in today's society. I believe that we deserve to be treated as economic equals in the human race. What's your opinion?

I think that subconsciously, men are jealous of women because they are feminine, can wear beautiful clothes, jewelry, makeup and sexy shoes and lingerie. They can bear children, nurse them with their breasts, and have complete license to express their emotions freely. Men are severely limited in many of those areas by our current standards. The freedom that men have that women do not is freedom to express their sexuality. Things tend to balance out when you look at it this way.

Why Men Tend to Dominate Women

A man looks upon his woman as his possession. He refers to his wife and she, her husband but what does that mean? When a man marries, he takes responsibility for the care and protection of that woman. It is something that is inherently passed on to him by tradition of what it is to be a man. Most men take their responsibility in that sense very seriously. Women do not think of their men as possessions, but traditionally more as a trophy. The subtlety of these traditions enhances the unspoken but implicit domination of men. It is so profound and accepted, that we don't even recognize it.

Women doctors are called nurses. Male nurses are called doctors. Waiters bring the bill to men. When shopping for cars, the salesmen address the men. I can go on forever with these illustrations but what do they prove? The bottom line is it exists. It has improved somewhat but it's not going to change at least not in our lifetime. So the only solution is to embrace it. It, being male dominance.

I think I have accepted the concept of male dominance. I am fine with men being in charge. Let them run the world. I don't need a woman president to feel complete. As long as women are present; we embrace our femininity and power as women; we bring our children into the world; we are the gatekeepers of sexuality, sensuality, and intimacy, men cannot survive without us. Women still are the only way that men can propagate the species. It is very interesting and amusing to observe men's initial reactions to my strategy. They object to the fact that the women are in charge of relationship. It seems that men want to be in charge of everything. They are immensely useful at solving problems and getting things done, however, when it comes to relating, communicating, and intimacy, they could use some remedial training.

Are You Ready to Get Engaged?

Planning a future with your man and testing your relationship to make sure that this person is 100% who you believe that he is, is the purpose of engagement. If you believe that you have found the person that you want to spend your life with, and you have decided to get married, then you both should be ready to set a date.

Setting a date for six to twelve months down the road is not just so you have time to order the flowers and find a band or reserve the church. An engagement period is the final discovery process to validate in every way that this is the person that you have chosen to live with for the next few decades.

Chemistry is probably the most frequently chosen criteria for choosing a mate. Having met someone with whom you have chemistry leads to comparing this person with the rest of your list. Agreement about money is a criterion. Men, for the most part, believe that they must be able to support their family. They do not want to take on the responsibility of another person and possibly children without achieving some sort of personal standard so that they can be the man in the family and provide the bread.

Do you share the same values and principals? Do you want to have children, and live in the same part of the country? Do you both balance your checkbook? What kind of house and lifestyle do you prefer? Marriage, as we define it today, is more of a business agreement than a passionate mating designed to bring offspring into the world. Our culture has designed weddings as ceremonial, and marriage as the business of raising children. In reality, everyone knows it's much more than that.

Women no longer expect to stay home and not work; however, they do not expect to be the better paid of the couple. How should one choose a mate? Unless you have done the necessary work to know who you are and what is important to you, you will not be able to choose a partner for the right reasons. Chemistry is rarely enough.

I have known so many couples who cannot stay away from each other because they are so turned on to each other, but the moment they are together outside of the bedroom, they disagree and fight about everything. Love conquers all is not necessarily a true statement. It depends on what you want along with the love.

If your priority is sex and money and his priority is success and security, there will be many arguments because you will not be well matched. If you want to travel and he wants to stay at home, there will be problems with logistics. When you consider a combination of chemistry, love, and the priorities in each other's lives, you have a much better chance of achieving success in your relationship.

What Don't You Understand About the Double Standard?

Women get pregnant but they are unable to do so without a man's sperm. So doesn't it follow that men get pregnant also? The double standard still prevails. It's only if the man gets caught that he has to assume responsibility for the pregnancy. Just because their bodies don't get misshapen doesn't mean that the child who is about to enter the world isn't his responsibility as well.

An unplanned pregnancy can create havoc in someone's world. Even now in this modern world we live in, when a woman gets pregnant, she is the one who endures the stigma, the physical discomfort, and the public awareness of her condition. The man can virtually go unnoticed throughout the entire pregnancy. Unless this man has integrity about fatherhood and this woman whom he has impregnated, he can literally walk away, publicly unscathed.

So what is it about the double standard that we don't understand? Women choose to get pregnant and men can choose to walk away? There is a certain amount of disconnect that occurs in relation to sexuality and parenthood. The whole concept parallels that of women no longer being sexual once they have become a mother or wife. While in this country, sex is flaunted in our faces at every moment in advertising; the actual attitude about sexuality is puritan. In other words, it's okay to talk about it, and joke about it, and use it to sell everything, but don't actually admit that you like to do it.

Scenario: What a Woman with Self-Esteem Can Accomplish

Keith and Julie have been dating for about six weeks. They were introduced by a relative of his and though they appear very mismatched, they seem to be having a good time together. Keith has been a wild-child party boy since his early teens. Julie is a sweet, unassuming young Certified Public Accountant (CPA). Keith has declared many times that he will never get married and never have children.

One day Keith tells his best friend that Julie is pregnant and his life is over. He is quite dramatic about it, stating he will not have a child and he will kill himself before he will agree to participate in anything having to do with Julie or her child. Meantime, Julie tells Keith she is having this baby with or without him. She continues with her life as if nothing special has occurred. Keith is reacting very badly to the whole situation. Julie doesn't flinch. She tells Keith that she will go to counseling with him so they can work this out. Keith is losing control.

Julie tells her parents that she is pregnant and having a child. She tells Keith's parents that they are going to be grandparents. Keith is still threatening dramatic actions to avoid any involvement.

Julie tells him she thinks they should get married. Keith says that they barely know each other. Julie doesn't waver. She continues to involve Keith in doctor's appointments, their ultrasound, and she makes an appointment for them to see a counselor.

This goes on for about six weeks. Keith continues to loudly protest any responsibility or involvement. Julie doesn't waver.

On or about the eighth week, Keith is still begging Julie to get an abortion. Julie tells him once and for all that she is having the baby, and that he is going to be a father whether he likes it or not. Whether he chooses to participate in the child's life, is up to him.

Keith finally consents to go to counseling, hoping that the counselor will side with him and tell Julie to give it up. The counselor tells Keith that he assumed the responsibility for this child the moment that he had unprotected sex with Julie, and that he really has no choice in the matter. The male counselor suggests that Keith rise to the occasion, and assume his responsibilities as a parent. Keith whines again to his buddy that he'd rather be dead.

Julie never wavers. She acknowledges Keith for his potential as a responsible partner and parent. She continues to state that she will have the child and that Keith will have to be responsible for his fatherhood. She enrolls them both for Lamaze classes.

Keith, under duress, accompanies Julie for an ultrasound, and when he recognizes his child has a heartbeat, he does an about-face. The next week, he shows up at his job and tells his buddy that he and Julie will be going to Lamaze classes, and that they are looking for a house to rent together.

One Year Later

Keith, Julie, and little Kevin are living together. Keith takes Kevin to and from day care every day and regales his co-workers with stories about his son. Keith and Julie are still in counseling. Keith, on occasion, laments how his life has changed, but he can't seem to stop bragging about his son's amazing accomplishments. Keith has been remodeling the house that they bought together and recently he bought Julie an engagement ring. They are still quite different in their approaches to life, but they seem to have balanced each other in many ways.

Scenario Analysis

Julie maintained her femininity and her power. She never wavered and continued to ask for what she wanted which was always much more than Keith thought he could produce. Julie was completely unwilling to settle, and simply acknowledged Keith, approved of him, and expected him to fulfill her "orders." Keith produced for her. He rose to her standards and they are now achieving a level of communication and intimacy that none of Keith's family or friends even suspected was possible for him. Keith is not unhappy. He glows with pride whenever he speaks about his son, and he seems to be seriously in love with Julie. They have had some very rocky times in the past year, but as long as Julie can continue providing challenges for Keith and approving of him, they have a chance for a successful long-term relationship.

This is not the best way to start a relationship. Unplanned pregnancies don't often increase a woman's self-esteem. It takes a woman who already has it to react the way that Julie did. Keith still has a way to go in his maturation process, but he has made heroic strides forward.

The double standard still exists, but women have the power to overrule it if they choose to do so. Keith may or may not be the right man for Julie, but she believes he is, and he rose to her challenges.

Involvement with Children—His and Hers

Attachment to someone else's children is a risk whenever you date someone who has them. There is a certain responsibility in being a parent and creating the legacy of morality and principals that you leave to your children as they journey through life. Is it fair to have children and let them get to know every person that you date on an intimate level? In an ideal world, people would meet, find the perfect partner, then mate, and create children of their own who would grow up and repeat the process. As we know, this is not a perfect world.

More than 50% of marriages end in divorce, and most of those marriages have created children who have no understanding of divorce or for that matter marriage. Children relate to people around them as if they are their family. Children actually see others as persons to love and who give affection and take care of them. When men and women enter each other's lives for the purpose of dating, it is honorable of them to consider the effect of their presence on the children. It is forever, even if it lasts only a few weeks.

Children can get in the way of an adult relationship, but for a parent, there can be no relationship without the involvement of their children. I know this absolutely wonderful guy who is raising three beautiful children by himself, and the bottom line is that he has no life without the kids. So, any woman who interests him will eventually have to meet, engage with, and enroll his children in order to have a relationship with him.

Consider protecting your children from your romantic involvements until you are fairly sure that it's going to be a long-term relationship. My rule of thumb, which is not written in stone, says: Don't involve the kids until you are sure you want this person in your life on a permanent basis. That would also be around the three-month mark, when you decide about sex. Kids are either a deal-breaker or deal-maker, but you really don't want to have a relationship only for the kids.

Are You Attracted to a Married Man?

Attraction to a married person is something that most people encounter at least once in their lives. It is appealing in many ways. First of all, you can remain fully independent and free of responsibility when you are having an affair with someone who is married. There is also a certain amount of security in terms of relationship risk. You always have a great excuse for why it didn't work. Ultimately, having a long-term relationship with a person who is married affords you some good and some bad things:

Bad news first:

- Your integrity is compromised
- Your credibility suffers
- You get to be alone on holidays and weekends
- You are 100% guaranteed that you will never come first in that person's life
- You usually get your heart broken.

Then the good news:

- You have a lot of free time
- You have great sex, when you have it
- You don't have to worry about that person taking too much money out of the ATM account
- You have freedom to pursue other interests
- You don't have to care about what you look like in the morning, because that person won't ever be there
- You really learn how to deal with disappointment
- You don't have to have a prenuptial agreement because there won't ever be any nuptials.

We asked my two-year-old grandson this question: "What does 'no' mean?" He responded: "Don't do it! Mommy said so." This would be good advice for those of you considering a relationship with a married man.

Choosing Your Ideal Mate

Matching up with someone who fits your preconceived idea of a mate is the preferred outcome of dating. If you subscribe to my strategy, checking on whether production is satisfactory by the man in the picture is another. Ultimately, it's the concept that you have to kiss a lot of frogs before you find a prince or princess. There is no denying, however, the wonderful feeling of falling in love and those first moments when you realize that this person standing opposite you is truly attracted and finds you desirable. It is an extraordinary feeling to be living your romantic fantasy.

It doesn't seem possible that there is any greater feeling on earth than feeling you are loved; that you are the special, personally-selected recipient of the most intimate and cherished feelings that this person has to share with you. That is the perfect outcome for dating.

Social status, appearance, likes and dislikes are all significant criteria for a marriage or committed relationship. The kind of relationship that I want to create and that I want for my clients to create is a relationship that fills the gaps in your soul. I want this person to compliment me in the areas where I am weak. I want him to love me with the passion that I love him. I want him to have as much, if not a little more, desire for sex than I have. I want him to have the same level of adventurousness, risk, challenge, excitement, and balance in his life that I do. I don't want him to be a mirror of myself, but I want him to challenge me in ways I have never considered, and to love and approve of me whether I succeed or fail in anything that I attempt.

Do You Want Marriage or a Business Merger?

When you choose a partner because his family has money and his company will merge well with yours, then you have committed to a business merger not a marriage. Marriage is a fluid state; it does not remain the same. It changes as the partners grow and mature. You have to be ready and willing to change with the flow of fate.

Life is a constant challenge and living with a partner is exponentially more challenging. Marriage is a choice. You can handle most things alone, but do you want to? I know that I do not want to spend my life taking care of everything by myself. I want a partner to share challenges, joys, rewards, excitement, difficulties, pleasure, love, and sex. I am not judging those who seek to marry for money, position, or power. It's just not what I am about and neither are the people who choose to work with me. I am looking for passionate people who want passion and pleasure in their lives no matter what.

Customs and Rituals

Tribal customs in ancient times dictated that women who did not attract a man were sacrificed. Thus, the desire and survival mechanism of, "I've got to have one or I'll die" arises from the cellular level of every woman. Some are more able to ignore it than others. It's more than the biological clock ticking away. It is a natural drive that is instinctual and cannot be replaced with anything else.

Recently, I read an article in People magazine about a woman in Nigeria who was sentenced to death by stoning for giving birth out of wedlock. The man she identified as the father was discharged for want of evidence. The execution of the sentence was postponed for eight months until the baby was weaned. She was not the first woman to be tried and convicted because she didn't have a man. This is an extreme. However, this discrimination and subtle domination of women exists commonly everywhere, even in our country and it simply goes unrecognized.

Men and women both want to be loved, approved of, and appreciated. My work is based on these truths. Neither work, nor career, nor children, nor homemaking can replace that level of satisfaction and fulfillment that arises in a woman when a man completely surrenders his love to her. I can only surmise that this is true for men as well. It is very difficult to describe the sensual pleasure and emotional freedom that results when a woman is sexually satisfied by a man who cherishes and adores her, and whom she trusts implicitly and loves enough to surrender to him.

I would imagine that a man who has a woman that he loves, willing to sexually surrender to him would be unequalled by any other male activities and pleasures. There is nothing else on earth that comes close to that ultimate pleasure. Those who have never experienced love in that manner have nothing else to compare it to; thus they will never know that they miss it.

Sexual Attraction

Energy that is created by sexual attraction along with the component of the mirror effect is what I believe romantic chemistry composition is all about. That kind of chemistry can exist for decades. That reminds me of a guy I met on the first day of high school and I was totally in love with him for four years. We never dated until after high school, but when we did, we became each other's first lovers and were together off and on sexually for several years before going our separate ways.

About 15 years later, a relative of mine married a relative of his. We ran into each other at a family event. We were both married at the time and I had three daughters by then. We spent the evening reminiscing about old high school friends, but the interesting part was that by the end of the evening, we were obviously turned on to each other.

We were accidentally, intentionally touching each other, moving closer and there was almost palpable energy flowing between us. It was, I believe, a superb demonstration of the power of chemistry. We could easily have forgotten our families and gone off to have passionate sex together, but we didn't. We saw each other again at our 30th high school reunion, and that energy resurfaced. It wouldn't surprise me if we would have the same reaction were we to meet again in our sixties.

Chemistry is very powerful and most likely is the source of love at first sight, and can certainly survive many years and trials if there are other compatibilities. I don't think that having only chemistry is enough to sustain a relationship, but it's why couples are attracted to each other. It is what is responsible for the attraction in those couples that you meet when you ask yourself, "What do they see in each other?"

Visibility, availability, and risk are the three things necessary for a man to get the woman he wants. First of all, since women do the choosing, he must get himself in front of the woman he desires so that she can notice him and give him the go-ahead signal. The next thing is that he must be available, which I define as being unattached, unmarried, capable of entering a relationship, and willing to do so. Of course, he must take the risk of rejection by making a move to engage the woman of his choice in conversation and eventually romantic interaction. He has to be willing to make a move.

Even though I say that women do the choosing, it looks like men do because they do the asking. Confusing? Of course it is. Romance is not straightforward and direct. I think that men would like it to be as simple as: "Me Man, You Woman, We Have Sex." Women, though, don't react well to such direct primal urges. Women believe that if a man wants sex, he should go for romance and seduction. He should indicate that he is attracted and pay attention to her. He should talk to her, and listen to her.

Women connect through conversation and before she will have sex with you, she needs to know that you regard her as more than a piece of ass. I do not believe that a woman can let go enough to orgasm until there is some trust with that man. That is not to say that a woman is never available for a one-night stand. However, if a woman will sleep with you the first time you ask, she has as much as dismissed you as a candidate for a long-term relationship. She has used you for sex.

Ironically, women demean men for one-night stands when it is actually always up to the woman if sex is going to occur. The one exception to that is rape. A woman needs to be reassured of several things, her attractiveness, that you actually care about her and her feelings, that you respect her and she needs to feel safe. A woman wants a man who makes her feel attractive as a woman and that she is respected as an intelligent life form.

Tradition has it that men do the choosing and that men take all the risk in establishing relationships with women. It is their ego and their macho tendencies, which lead them to these conclusions. They do take a risk in asking a woman for a date. However, men who pay attention to women and who pay attention to the signals that they receive from women will know when it is safe to proceed.

I believe that chemistry and physical attractiveness play a part in attraction, but, more than anything else, it is a woman's perception of a man's ability to produce results that will get him noticed. That's why it isn't always the best-looking guys who get the best-looking girls. Once you reach a certain age level, it isn't what someone looks like that matters. It is how they function in the world and how well they play with others.

When men accept that women do the choosing, they recognize that they must do something to get noticed and approved of, before they will get chosen. Women never get over the belief that it is their attractiveness that will get them a man. Unfortunately, that is a woman's weakness. She will always begin doubting her attractiveness. It is the first thing that a woman will ever consider when she feels dumped by a man. She'll think to herself, "I wasn't pretty, sexy or thin enough." If this is really true, he didn't deserve to have her.

Men rarely think it's their looks that get them women. Even the most attractive and unattractive men don't think first about whether they are attractive enough. They might consider their height, but how many men who have huge noses get nose jobs? The exception to that rule might be actors in

Hollywood, who are not normal men. I have actually seen a man get on a scale in front of a roomful of co-workers and announce that he had gained thirty pounds without a second thought as to how he would be perceived. What woman do you know who could do something like that? Men will doubt their ability to produce results for the woman that they have chosen. That is their vulnerable spot.

Love, chemistry, and compatibility are the three components necessary to have a good match. I believe that all three are essential ingredients for long-term relationship. If you have love and compatibility you can be very good friends but without the chemistry there will be no passion. If you have chemistry and compatibility but no love, you can be on the same path and have great sex but you will grow to hate each other. If you have love and chemistry but no compatibility, you will outgrow each other and eventually be in separate places. However, if you have all three, you can grow together, try new paths, have passion, and with love, you can express the vulnerability that is necessary to survive a long-term relationship.

So how do you find someone who has the compatibility, the love, and the chemistry that will make a relationship work? It isn't easy. The compatibility issue is the tricky part because it's imperative that you are in synch with each other. For example, it wouldn't work for someone in their forties who still wants children of their own to engage with someone who's already a grand-parent and has absolutely no intention of having another child.

The same conflict would exist, for example, if someone who is 54, wanted to retire at age 55, met someone who was just starting a new business and wanted to work long hours. Religion, culture, age, children, parents, animals, career paths, geography, history, drugs, alcohol and cigarette use, sexual needs, and even astrological signs can sometimes enter into the compatibility screening. I'm not saying that any of these things are disqualifiers; they are simply things to consider.

Scenario: Don't Settle for Less than What You Really Want

After several years of living single and dating various men, Hope, age 40, finally meets Mark, a man she is attracted to, who has been in her circle of friends for several years. Independently, each of them has committed to going on a cruise with that same group of friends. While on the cruise, they spent a lot of time together and started seeing each other regularly after the cruise.

Mark appears to have everything Hope has described on her list for her ideal man, with two seemingly minor differences. Hope is a born-again Christian, and Mark believes in God but is non-denominational and doesn't attend church. Hope loves to dance and Mark tolerates it. They date seriously for two years, and he meets and engages with her three children from a former marriage. Mark is an only child and lives with his mother. They discuss marriage.

Hope

Mark, you are so much the man I have wanted in my life. You are kind, generous, and loving. You are successful in your business and I am very attracted to you. The only thing that I would request of you is that you be more spiritually connected, and I'm not sure that we're on the same wave length spiritually. When we first started dating, you said you believed in God, but you don't have a personal relationship with God, it's more of an intellectual relationship.

Mark

I believe in God and I don't know what else you expect of me in that respect.

Hope

If you can just get your relationship with God out of your head and into your heart, I would spend the rest of my life with you.

Mark

I'll try. (Another six months passes and Mark has not embraced Christianity, nor has he proposed to Hope. His excuse is that he doesn't know what to do with his mother because he takes care of her.)

Hope

Mark, I don't think that this is going to work between us, and I want to end our relationship. Your commitment to God is missing for me, and as perfect as you are in every other way, I am not willing to sacrifice my belief in Christ to be with you.

Mark

I've been expecting a conversation about this lately because I've sensed that you are not really content with everything between us. It's really because you love country dancing and I hate it, isn't it?

Hope

No, Mark, it's the spirituality that you don't grasp. I could probably handle your mother, and the issues with dancing, but I can't accept that we are not on the same spiritual path. I know that you don't really understand this, but if you did, it wouldn't be an issue. I love you but that is not enough. I am going to stop seeing you.

Scenario Analysis

This is an example of the very difficult situation where Mark was almost perfect for Hope, yet she knew something was missing. Many women would have been unwilling to give him up for fear of not finding another man who is a better match. Hope took a big risk by dismissing Mark. The easy thing to do would have been to settle on Mark accepting that he would just not be compatible spiritually. She chose the more difficult route and dismissed him. These situations are the most challenging.

When someone is almost perfect, the tendency is to settle, convincing yourself that it will work itself out, but in fact it never does. That one thing becomes the issue that destroys the relationship. Hope has now begun a relationship with another man who is spiritually aligned with her, and in addition, he loves to dance. Hope has attained the level of self-esteem necessary to trust her intuition and come from a place of abundance, knowing that God and the universe will provide someone equal or better.

Hope found that it was very difficult to end her relationship with Mark because he was so close to what she had wanted. This is one of those situations where love is not enough. She could have settled, but she didn't. Hope got the courage to dismiss Mark because he couldn't meet her most valued standard.

Testing Your Appetite

Passion is not the only reason for relationship. Companionship, security, financial stability, and adventure can also motivate people to make the commitment. Personally, I think passion is the best reason, but there are probably many people around the world who would passionately disagree with me. What if intimate relationships exist partially to heal old traumas?

It is inevitable that "personal stuff" will come up for each person which disrupts the momentum of a relationship. At that time, each person can choose what to do with the "stuff" that causes the reaction. Multiple choices exist:

- You can choose to blame the incident on whoever is in front of you

- You can ignore the situation completely

- You can separate the reaction from the incident and look to see if your reaction is appropriate for the situation

- If the reaction is out of proportion from the incident, you can then choose to look for the cause of the reaction which will be somewhere in your past

- At that moment, you have an opportunity for intimacy with your partner

- You can continue to rage about the current incident knowing full well that it's not the real problem

- You can choose to delve into the original incident, sharing it with your partner and then search for the opportunity to heal while deepening your connection with your partner.

It's up to you. Of course, there are going to be incidents that occur during a relationship that must be dealt with in real time, and they will bring up emotions from things in the past. You can deal with the present and still have choices about the past and the level of intimacy which you would like to attain with your partner.

Test your appetite and see what kind of response you get from the man you have chosen. If he produces for you, it validates that he will produce for you some of the time. Please understand this is not about controlling or manipulating a man. Men are strong-willed, independent-thinking, totally self-sufficient creatures. They certainly do not need a woman to tell them what to do. However, once a man has chosen you to love and cherish, and you have committed to each other, someone must steer the relationship boat. If no one does, your relationship will flounder, and it will have no direction.

Many relationships exist this way and for the most part nothing serious will result. Women care about relationship. Although men care if their life is comfortable and runs smoothly, they really are not interested in the fine workings of a relationship. They just want to be happy and have you be happy, too. They have other things on their mind. So if you want your relationship to continue to grow and thrive, for the most part, you as the woman will have to steer it.

The list that you made awhile ago about the person you wanted to show up in your life, required that you trusted in the universe to deliver, and that you had true clarity about your desires. The power of attraction is a subject onto itself, and actually has been addressed by many more qualified than me. For further research, you can refer to Thomas Leonard and his Principles of Attraction tapes. Manifesting 101, by Susan James, is another resource for learning how to get what you want. However, just as in the realm of relationship, be careful what you ask for, because you just might get it.

You must love yourself before you can love anyone else. This is the challenge that comes with relationship. Ultimately, everyone out in front of you is merely a reflection of yourself. You can only see what you already know. Using the attraction principles can bring you a life that you have designed for yourself.

Change is what happens to relationships. They do not end. Only upon death do they appear to be finally ended, but many continue to receive the benefits, the frustrations, and the legacy of that bond even after death. Relationships are infinite. They never end. They simply change form.

The "How to Get What You Want from Your Man Anytime" Strategy

- Be direct.

- Acknowledge him graciously and honestly.

- Use your appetite to ask for EXACTLY what you want.

- Ignore his hesitation and objections.

- Recognize when he violates one of your MAJOR standards and never settle.

- When he produces the result you want, show your appreciation.

- Dismiss him completely when he doesn't produce for you.

Chapter 6
Sex—The Foundation of Intimacy

"Most women would rather keep their men and fake pleasure than take the risk of telling the truth and having their men leave."
—Ron Smotherman, *Transforming #1*

Having enough sex is not a concept that men understand. Sex is a primal urge and the first and last thought of the day for most men. The general consensus is that men will do anything for sex. They are consumed with the idea as can be verified by looking at any advertisement and media that exists in this country. We are inundated by sexual innuendo and blatant sexual ads. The entertainment industry is driven by sex and most of the entertainment industry is run by men.

A man's most likely reason for getting into a relationship is for the purpose of getting sex. The pornography business is in existence because men keep it profitable. Most pornography is designed around the act of sex. There is not seduction, not sensuality, not foreplay and certainly not cuddling after sex. I have said to my director friend, that the capture of an authentic orgasm by a woman on film would be the most seductive pornography on the market.

Erotic thoughts are not foreign to women. Although women lean more towards love and emotional involvement, women like sex as much as men do. Women however, are hesitant to exhibit their true appetite for sex because they fear that their level of desire will intimidate men. Women also resist being the aggressor in sex because they don't want to appear to be too experienced.

"Oral Gratification—There are really only two ways to satisfy an insatiable appetite and one of them involves food."
—Author Unknown, *Instyle magazine*

To women, sex is more than just intercourse. It is romance, seduction, sensuality, mood, touching, intimacies, and many times, love. It is a known fact that women attach much more emotion to sex than men do. I don't think a woman will sexually surrender to a man unless she trusts him. That doesn't mean that every woman who has sex with a man, trusts him. Sexual surrender is a whole subject onto itself, but for these purposes let's say that there are many levels of surrender when it comes to sex and intimacy for women. Most women would choose to have sex and love in the same package if they could get it.

To men, sex means they get to come, which means orgasm which also means they need to have an erection, which means they have to produce it. When a man is seventeen, this is never a problem. When they get older, it can be. So when a woman says I want to spend a weekend in bed with you, it can strike terror into the minds of a lot of men. To men, sex and love are entirely separate. I think they have separate circuitry in their brains and if they happen to get sex and love at the same time, it can short circuit their brains. Okay, remember I said there would be a lot of generalizations in this book? This is one of them.

Someone told me that women need a reason for sex and men just need a place. As I have said before in this book, men and women are different. The bottom line is that women are in charge of sex. They get to decide when, where, and for how long the sexual encounter will continue, and if it will ever happen again.

The Madonna Complex

The Madonna complex is a state of mind that men carry about women and their relationship to sex. Everyone judges women who are easy, to be sluts. Women let men run cover for them about sex because it is just not socially acceptable for women to be blatant with their sexuality. Men want their woman to be sexy and seductive but only to them. If the woman is too sexy, other men might notice and then make a judgment that their woman is a slut.

If the woman is too conservative, other men might think their woman is frigid. So the woman bears the obligation to be sexy but not seductive with other men. This is a very fine line. Every man wants other men to envy him, but he doesn't want the other men to try to move in on him with his sexy woman. Women, therefore, end up walking a very tight line and many times being very confused. It is not compatible to be a slut, a mother, and a wife at the same time. So the idea of having a woman take on the role of being a slut in the bedroom and a respectable wife and mother the rest of the time is what the Madonna complex is all about. Some men cannot get over the fact that their sexy woman has become a mother and it interferes with their sex life for the rest of their marriage.

Teaching Men to be Great Lovers

Experience creates great male lovers. Wrong! The macho influence causes most men to believe that they are great lovers along with the lies that they are told by the women who love them. What do I mean? Well, looking at the way that men learn about sex, how can they be anything but great lovers? They learn from girly magazines and bragging in the locker room and porno flicks. What do they learn there? They certainly do not learn the art of seduction and sensuality.

Why don't women teach men how to be great lovers? I believe that it's mostly because they lack self-esteem in the area of their bodies and its functions. Women, for the most part, are ashamed that they cannot be aroused and orgasm as quickly as men do. They learn when they are teenagers that men can get turned on by anything and essentially are walking erections when they are seventeen. They reach orgasm very quickly while a woman requires foreplay, seduction and some very direct attention to various parts of her body. Most women do not have the nerve to instruct a man and they get embarrassed because it takes him so long to figure out how to make her come. So women lie. They fake orgasms to make their men feel good about how they are making love. A woman fakes an orgasm to make her man feel proud of his performance. It's easier to lie about an orgasm and her satisfaction than it is to rouse her tired self enough to tell the truth and teach a man.

A woman's self-esteem is at stake, along with the man's macho ego. A woman wants a man to think that she does not know much about sex, because especially in the beginning, she wants him to think that she is a virgin or close to it. So it all stems from the fact that it is not socially acceptable for women to know about sex.

It is all ridiculous, because neither men nor women when they are young know the first thing about sex, arousal, and orgasms except by accident, unless someone teaches them. So, who is going to teach them? Certainly their parents won't teach them because they can barely provide the knowledge of body function and sexual reproduction. Sex education classes deal with the anatomy and physiology of sex, and the mechanical act, but who deals with teaching children about the emotions, and psychological stamina for sex? Who teaches young people about seduction, sensuality, and making love instead of having sex, sexual surrender and the level of intimacy required to achieve it? No one. So everyone learns by default.

It's no wonder we have so many men and women being bad lovers, and so many lovers having bad relationships. Many marriages fail because both parties are bad at sex and relationship. Unless one of them was fortunate enough to have someone with experience teach them about arousal, seduction, and love and sensuality, neither knows anything. Understand this: many women go their entire lives without ever experiencing good sex. Truthfully, so do many men. When men think that their own orgasm constitutes good sex, they don't realize that a male orgasm is just the beginning, and they can do that by themselves without any emotional involvement.

The fragility of a man's ego can lead to impotence and ultimately the exit of a man from a woman's life. This is a common belief that women have about men and sex. Women are afraid to tell a man the truth about their experience of sex because they are afraid that it will send the man away. They are also afraid to tell a man the truth about their level of enjoyment of sex because they fear judgments about their level of experience.

If a woman has the arrogance to attempt to teach a man how to make love to her, then he might think that she thinks that he has no experience at all. The bottom line fear that women have about telling a man the truth about sex is that if she tells him that she likes sex and wants sex as much or more than he does, she will intimidate him and scare him away for good.

Most men believe that women want him to produce an erection which will provide hours of uninterrupted sexual contact. This is not true, but these are the common beliefs that get in the way of even the most experienced and accomplished lovers.

The other day I heard a 50-year-old man make a comment to a woman who had asked him to go away for a weekend of nothing but sex. He said that he couldn't provide such a performance although he had lots of experience. So it seems they never learn. The whole problem about sex in relationships has evolved into the most complicated, dishonest, assumptive, mess on everyone's part, mainly because no one will tell the truth about sex.

Women bring fullness to life, passion into relationships, and intimacy into sex. For men, sex can be an act, devoid of emotion, and it can be about pure physical pleasure only. It takes a woman to lead a man into full sexual surrender and the experience of passion and intimacy that is available only to those who are willing to risk losing everything they have in order to get what they want. A man who surrenders to a woman's power in relationship will reap rewards he does not even know that he doesn't know exist.

Boredom, cheating, and avoiding sex in a relationship is the result of women tolerating bad sex. What is bad sex? It's repetitive, unimaginative, and non-orgasmic sex for women. Women are creative and imaginative. They thrive on unexpected pleasure. Most people love surprises and surprises in seduction are no exception.

Imagine a woman having a lover who gets an erection, and simply wants to sex her long enough to get off. This is the reality of sexual intercourse for many uneducated and inexperienced women and men. Hopefully, sex education has at least taught them that the organ which causes a woman's pleasure, is not located within the vagina; that it will take more than just intercourse for her to reach orgasm. Unfortunately for many women, sex never gets beyond simple intercourse and to them it is just bad sex, a wifely obligation.

Many men wonder why their women do not react the way the porno stars act. The key term here is "act" which is what the porn "actresses" do. A lot of men learn how to make love by watching those porn films, which provides a great explanation as to why many men have such deplorable love-making techniques. Then again, there is a huge difference between having sex and making love, and porn is all about having sex. There is no thought of love in those films.

Once in awhile, a woman who has never had good sex, gets to experience it, and then the trouble begins. Why? It's because she will want more good sex, and it's likely that the good sex that she experienced wasn't with her regular partner. It's likely that the regular partner learned about sex from pornography and she never had the nerve to teach him anything different.

Truly, it is not all the man's fault. He just doesn't know any better because no one has taught him differently. I have heard from many women that when they first engaged in sexual activity, they had no idea what it was supposed to be like, good or bad. Therefore, they can't begin to ask for what they want, because they don't know.

Intimacy in a Relationship

The drama surrounding the sexual relations of a married couple does not support intimacy in their relationship. On the contrary, the sexual habits of most married couples lead to the greatest distance between them. After a woman has tolerated being used for sex for many years, and after a man has tolerated what he views as unresponsiveness from his woman for many years, a woman will create a huge upset and avoid sex all together.

I once had a conversation with a prominent physician (I'll call him Bill) on a long flight to Europe about the subject of sex.

Bill

Women lose interest in sex as they got older and nearer to menopause.

Susan

Your attitude surprises me. I completely disagree with you. What makes you think that way?

Bill

It's been my experience, personally.

Susan

Are you married?

Bill

I am.

Susan

Where's your wife and why didn't she accompany you on your trip to Italy?

Bill

She's home with our three children.

Susan

Wouldn't she have loved to visit Italy with you during your medical conference?

Bill

Our children's ages are two, five, and eight. She needed to stay home to take care of them. Don't get me wrong. She's really a great mother and she even nursed each child for three years. But she's not interested in sex.

Susan

It seems to me that for the past nine years, she has either been pregnant or nursing a child. Answer this for me then. Was she ever a happy slut in the bedroom?

Bill

Yes, she was.

Susan

Then you might want to consider that she still could be, if you gave her a reprieve from motherhood and house slavery.

What does this typical conversation prove? It shows that men are unconscious about what it takes to nurse and mother a child, let alone three children. Men are also unconscious about how women feel about sex. Granted, there are many women who really don't care if they ever have sex again, but I would venture a guess that these are the women who have never experienced wonderful, orgasmic, spiritually-connected sex.

Puritan Ethics

Our puritan ethic creates guilt around the idea of any excess. People in this country suffer from resistance to pleasure. It is common for adults to feel guilty when things are going too good. Too much pleasure is considered sinful. It is flaunted in our faces by every advertiser, but when it comes to actual acceptance of pleasure as a way of life; it is judged by many to be excessive.

We have a strong work ethic and puritan roots. However, many of us were raised to believe that we must work harder in order to be successful. Prove it by checking out yourself.

When do you give yourself permission to just enjoy pleasure without guilt? How often do you say, "I should be doing this or that" when you are enjoying yourself? We start teaching our children early to forego pleasure by repeating phrases such as: "No pain. No gain." "Put your nose to the grindstone." "Work harder." "People who work smart are con artists."

Men do not acknowledge their ignorance regarding a woman's body, or their own capacity to love. If you want a man to be good in bed, women, you must teach him. Approve of him and acknowledge him sincerely. Give him an order (like from a menu) and follow it up with another acknowledgement of how well he performed your order. Repeat as needed and remember: men are slow learners and need much repetition.

Men will recognize that this training is tantamount to staying after school to learn how to make love. Men do not know women's bodies. Unfortunately, many women do not know their own bodies. If a woman wants a good lover, she must first learn her own body responses, and then teach them to the man she loves. Remember, a man wants to please his woman, especially sexually. It is a real accomplishment to give a woman an orgasm that she will never forget.

A woman cannot surrender completely to a man she does not trust. Men want to hear and see and feel their women orgasm. The louder it is, the more they like it. It strokes their ego. The idea of making a woman scream is really what arouses most men. They will continue to learn, explore, and experiment, if the woman is willing.

Erotic Fantasies

Erotic fantasies bring pleasure to both parties. The result of honesty in sexual intimacy is that it is an aphrodisiac. Telling a man about your fantasy and giving him the opportunity of creating it and participating in it are some of the most erotic actions that a woman can provide for her man. The same is true for men and their fantasies. If they feel open enough to share a true erotic fantasy with a woman, and she grants him the privilege of sharing its experience with her, provided they do not cross any of either's moral values, they both achieve greater intimacy.

Telling the truth about sex is more erotic than any pornography. It is a pleasure that most are resistant to trying, out of fear and possibly a little guilt due to that puritan ethic of ours. I have acted out several of my own fantasies with a lover and sometimes it proved to be more enjoyable than the fantasies. In other cases, it wasn't as much fun as the fantasy but then you win some and you lose some, so why not try anyway? As long as you don't cross any vital boundaries, fantasy in lovemaking is a real aphrodisiac. I have had clients tell me how they go to bars with their lovers to pick up on other men, just so he can watch, even though there is never any intention to follow through. It is the intent which creates the passion.

Sensuality and anticipation of pleasure contribute to arousal. Interestingly, men cannot turn on by themselves. They require a woman's stimulus in order to get aroused. Men get their pleasure from a woman's body. They derive their pleasure from giving pleasure to their woman. A woman, however, can turn on by herself anytime she pleases.

The Man's Sexual Goal

The greatest goal of any heterosexual man is to cause a woman to orgasm, to lose control, to completely surrender to him and his sexuality. Orgasm is about surrender. Thus, a woman will guard her orgasm and possibly fake one with a man that she does not trust.

It is a man's job to fill up a woman not just literally but to saturate her sexually. What goes unknown is that a woman has a huge sexual capacity. She can take an extensive amount of sexing before she is saturated and satisfied. Thus, most women never get completely satisfied. Because men think that sexing is only intercourse and receiving head, the things you see in porno flicks, whereas women think sexing is anything sensual, sexual, foreplay, flirting, touching, tenderness, and the intimacy that follows intercourse, in addition to actual sexual acts.

There is a huge gap in satisfaction between the sexes. Of course, one weekend shared between a woman who knows about real sexing, and a man who is willing to learn, will open both of their minds and expand their comfort zones. Their pleasure will only be inhibited by their individual limitations revolving around surrender.

The Mental Sexuality

Men are very visual and women secrete pheromones, which cause sexual turn on. Sexuality is primarily in the mind of both and therefore it is most important for women to accept and display their sexuality. I'm not referring to a woman looking slutty, but rather for her to feel her sexuality from within her own body. A woman who has the self-esteem to know that she is feminine, powerful, attractive, loving, sensual, and charming, can walk into a room and feel everyone in the room responding to her. This is the place that I strive to take all of my female clients.

It doesn't actually matter whether she has the perfect body or the most expensive clothing. What really matters is her energy and how she presents it. A woman who knows her power can do this. It is what makes her attractive to both sexes. She can choose any man she wants. Men have radar for women who are capable of these vibrations.

Men have this power as well, and what attracts a woman to a man is his ability to produce results. I know you have heard me say this before but it isn't looks that create the attraction for women. Men are more visual and are initially attracted by visual stimuli, such as a woman's body and how she carries herself. But the final attraction comes from the energy and the self-esteem that is projected by both.

Exploring New Sexual Horizons

Inhibitions have very little place in sexual encounters. Sex is the most fun that anyone can have for free. There is a certain amount of risk in every sexual meeting, but each encounter can create growth and expansion of the comfort zone of each person. We all grow up with certain beliefs and limitations, however, my mind-set is that sexual intimacy between two people who love and trust each other should not be limited by beliefs or any limitations. It takes trust to overcome long-lasting limitations and that is what long-term sexual relationships are about. They help each partner explore new horizons, reach new levels of pleasure, and build a foundation for trust and intimacy that never existed prior.

I do believe that sex is a doorway to intimacy between couples. One must be vulnerable enough to engage in sexual play and to take risks and surrender to each other. It is not without risk when establishing a new sexual relationship, but life is about risk and the only cost of sex is the cost of your self-esteem. If you choose the wrong partner, that partner will not cherish your intimacy as the most sacred gift.

One common fantasy that most men and some women have is a threesome. I want to make a statement here regarding this. If you are open to this, go ahead and try it, but be aware that it is not likely to increase intimacy or the bond between a couple. In fact, it can be the seed for some serious disruption and destruction in a relationship. Each of you needs to define your own limits when it comes to sexual freedom. Playing with this fantasy, exploring the idea of it, even going so far as suggesting partners to each other does nothing more than titillate the senses and make the sexual experience more enjoyable.

Participating in an actual threesome (or more) can result in some surprise reactions that you weren't expecting in your intimate relationship. I guess what I am saying here is never consent to anything that you really don't want to do, just to please your partner. Differentiate between sex as recreation and sex for the purpose of intimacy. Draw the lines that you won't cross before you are in the situation to avoid having to decide on the spot. No one can think clearly in the throes of passion.

One way to really play with men's heads and many times put a stop to the fantasy if you so desire is to suggest that turn-about is fair play and you might consider a threesome if it is two men and you and everyone participates with everyone. I did this once in an extended conversation about sex that took place in one of those employment places that had a sexual free zone. One man never forgave me for putting that visual in his brain. Months later I saw him and it was the first comment out of his mouth. He suggested that I was bad to have even conceived of such an idea.

It's not up to me to suggest limits on sexuality and I hope you understand that whatever you choose to do sexually with your partner behind doors is completely your choice. Your safety is what matters, so be discriminating with your choices of both men and limits. .

Women, please remember: It is always your responsibility to set the limits, and if a man does not respect those limits, it is rape.

Sex is irreversible. You cannot ever go back to not having had sex with a person. That sounds obvious however, think about what it means. Taking proper precautions anywhere and anytime on any days or nights that you choose to have sex will not protect you from the changes which occur when you surrender your body to another person. When you choose to get to know someone and you participate in sex after only a few hours, it changes your relationship. The result is that you can never again return to that state that you were in prior to engaging in sex with that person.

If you choose to delay sexual desires and put off having sexual intimacy until you learn about that person, you will see a whole different person. So the cost of premature sexual intercourse is enormous. You give up knowing who that person is without the sexual overtones. You might even give up the opportunity to learn to love this person, because everything is altered once that boundary has been crossed.

I encourage my clients to refrain from sexual intimacy for at least three months of intense interaction so that the values and beliefs of each person can be explored to check for compatibility. Although the sexual energy might be present, it doesn't mean that the two persons are completely attracted to each other and compatible as lovers and partners.

Too many times I have witnessed incredible sexual attraction, energy, and satisfaction without the substance of compatible friendship, love, and respect for each other. Relationships like these usually end in divorce. So give yourself a chance to know this person if you are serious about having a long-term relationship with sexual intimacy.

When I say the foundation of intimacy is sex, it is not the first stone but the final stone of the foundation after all the relationship groundwork has been done.

Scenario: Don't Be Fooled When It's Too Easy

Gina, age 28, has been exclusively dating Craig, age 30, for four months. They have chemistry. They have a lot of things in common, and Gina thinks she's in love with Craig. Gina has decided she's ready to have sex with him to verify that they really are compatible, and the following conversation ensues:

Gina

Since we met, I have been continually impressed with your values and your integrity as a man. I also told you repeatedly that I was looking for a serious relationship leading to marriage.

Craig

(Who is kissing her neck and working on seducing her.) I said I was ready for some of that. So what's up?

Gina

I just want to make sure that you know that that's what I want.

Craig

And I want you. So let's go to bed.

Gina

Okay. (Gina believes she has done everything right up to this point.)

They have sex. At the end of their evening, he invites her to a reunion with some old college friends. Next evening at a restaurant bar, when Gina arrives, Craig is talking with another woman. He stops long enough to introduce her to everyone, get her a drink and then returns his attention to the other woman. She feels ignored and this upsets her. She goes to the bathroom to sort out her thoughts and feelings. When she returns, he is dancing with the other girl. She takes her purse and walks out the door. He notices that she's leaving. He follows her. And they have the following conversation in the parking lot.

Craig

Hey Gina. Wait a minute. Where are you going?

Gina

I'm going home.

Craig

Why? What's wrong? I thought we were having a good time.

Gina

You were having a good time with that girl. Your friends were all having a good time with each other. The Bartender was having a good time selling lots of drinks, but I was not having a good time at all.

Craig

Well, if you would join in the conversation and fun, it might be fun for you too. You don't expect me to be with you 100% of the time, do you? This is not a date, you know.

Gina

I came here to be with you, not exclusively, but you have ignored me completely since I got here. You are all over that Katie and I was sitting alone. That is not what I expected from you.

Craig

What is it that you want and what are you getting at?

Gina

I want a serious committed relationship. I want to get married.

Craig

Well, I don't.

Gina stares at him; her expression evolving from shock to reality. At that moment, she recognizes that she has been in denial about Craig's level of commitment to her. She has been hearing what she's wanted to hear, and not the truth.

Gina

Okay, Craig. Good-bye. (Gina gets in her car and drives away).

Scenario Analysis

At that moment, Gina recognized that he had been stroking her ego and telling her only what she wanted to hear. It was only then that Gina could comprehend that Craig's intentions, comments, and attention had been directed at getting her cooperation in her own seduction. Gina became aware that his values and integrity regarding women, specifically her, were not what she wanted. She realized that he did not deserve to have her. And it became easy for her to instantly dismiss him.

This is a case where it was probably necessary for Gina to have taken the step to include sexual intimacy for her to then learn Craig's beliefs and attitude about women and sex. Gina had been honest about her intentions, and Craig had used those intentions to achieve a notch on his sexual scorecard by purposely clouding his responses to her. Gina, in her anxiousness to find a mate, had ignored all the warning signs by not listening to what he was saying.

The "How to Get What You Want from Your Man Anytime" Strategy

- Be direct.

- Acknowledge him graciously and honestly.

- Know what you want and ask for EXACTLY what you want.

- Ignore his hesitation and objections because men always say no at first. If he doesn't say no, be wary of him telling you what you want to hear just to get what he wants

- Recognize when he violates one of your MAJOR standards and never settle.

- Dismiss him completely when he doesn't produce for you.

Chapter 7
Life is Not a Fairy Tale

"You can hold a reel of film in your hands and it's all finished and complete–beginning, middle, end are all there that same second, the same millionths of a second. The film exists beyond the time that it records, and if you know what the movie is, you know generally what's going to happen before you walk in to the theatre: there's going to be battles and excitement, winners and losers, romance, disaster; you know that's all going to be there. But in order to get caught up and swept away in it, in order to enjoy it to its most, you have to put it in a projector and let it go through the lens minute by minute...any illusion requires space and time to be experienced."
—Richard Bach, *Illusions*

From a very young age, children learn about fairy tales, and watch television or go to the movies where relationships are portrayed with "happily ever after" endings. Prior to reality television, most shows were based on the Ozzie and Harriet, Leave it to Beaver family model. Even the Huxtables, and the Keatons were fairy tale material. These shows set the stage for women to believe that their family lives would be the same. Pretty Woman is an example of the modern fairy tale. Not that hookers will marry rich guys, but that the fairy tale begins when you marry the prince. In reality, there is no such thing as happily ever after. Unfortunately, those stories are responsible for the failure of many marriages. Things just don't happen the way they do on television or in the movies.

Scenario: Career Women Get Tempted by Married Men

Katharine is attracted to Jack, a married man who works in her office and is indirectly her superior. He plays with her by e-mail, writing amusing notes and side comments. Jack's wife lives in another city, and he commutes on weekends. Katharine is a powerful and successful business woman; however, she has never had a long-term, romantic relationship. In fact, she doesn't know how to go about starting one.

During one of their business parties at a local bar, Jack and Katharine have drinks together and talk. By the end of the evening, he walks her to her car, and in a moment of weakness, kisses her good night. Jack immediately recognizes that he is in dangerous waters and retreats. Katharine is even more attracted to him now and decides that he is probably getting divorced and could be available for her. The next day, they have the following phone conversation.

Jack

Hi, how are you?

Katharine

Fine.

Jack

About last night . . .

Katharine

I know.

Jack

I'm married and whether I stay married or not depends on how things turn out in the future.

Katharine

I understand.

Jack

I'm very attracted to you but I wouldn't want to put you in a compromising position. I've been married for 20 years and have never done anything like this before and it wouldn't be right to involve you.

Katharine

Well, can't we just be friends? You sound like you could use a friend.

Jack

Sure.

Scenario Analysis

Several things occurred and didn't occur in this conversation. First of all, they did not discuss what happened or what the flirtatious encounter meant to either of them. Jack did not reveal the status of his marriage or what he intended to do about either his marriage or Katharine.

Jack made a vague statement about his marriage which could mean anything from he is happily married and wants to stay that way, to 'I am out the door at home and can't wait to leave.'

Likewise, Katharine didn't say anything. She didn't express any appetite. She didn't make it clear that she was not interested in having any kind of a relationship with a married man. She made several assumptions: 1) that he was on the verge of divorce; 2) that he would want to have an affair; and 3) that he didn't want to have an affair with her. She was willing to settle for being a friend and having any kind of a relationship at all because she was so attracted to him.

So what is real in this scenario?

- Jack is attracted

- Jack is married

- Jack is flattered by the attention

- Jack would like to proceed but has some integrity, so he won't

- Katharine is attracted

- Katharine has little experience in relationships
- Katharine is available
- Katharine would like to proceed

Why? (Supposition only)

- Jack's marriage is not as solid as it could be
- Any man would be flattered by attention from an attractive powerful woman
- Jack doesn't want to cheat on his wife
- Katharine is attracted to Jack because he pays attention to her not because of who he is, because she doesn't know him well enough
- Katharine decides Jack is rejecting her because he is not attracted to her; not because he has any integrity in his marriage
- Katharine does not have the self-esteem to ask for what she wants, which is a relationship with an available man.

So why is it that as women we believe in fairy tales? Because that's all there is. Look around. How many happy marriages do you see? From my perspective, I don't see that many. I see a lot of people tolerating each other for the sake of something else. That "something" could be children, finances, family, or security. How many do I see absolutely reveling in the joy of being together? On rare occasions, I see a couple who truly thrive on each other. Why is this so rare? I think it's because people don't know how to have a thriving relationship.

Unrealistic Expectations

The expectation that a relationship will be just like the fairy tale or the TV show exists, but very few know how to achieve that level of compatibility. Reality gets in the way. Women expect that men know how they want to be treated. Men expect women to be emotional and dramatic. Neither person communicates their true wants and needs to each other, so everyone operates in a vacuum and the connection is lost.

There is no such thing as "happily ever after." There only is "now." The present moment is all there is, and one look at the obituaries will prove that. So how do you experience the present moment, and communicate your love and respect to those you are in relationship with? Telling the truth is a good start, and it begins by not fooling yourself with lies and idealism.

In reality, modern fairy tales still exist. A man wants and expects a virgin princess who will wait on him hand and foot, who will have sex with him on demand, and who will support his every thought and deed. The problem with that fantasy is there aren't too many virgins out there, and the women in the world have other thoughts about waiting on men hand and foot and what their fate should be.

Men also seem to believe that wives and mothers should be sex goddesses in the bedroom. Nothing wrong with this thinking except that being a wife, mother and having a job which most women do these days makes you tired. In fact, we're too tired to become a sex goddess every night. So where does that leave men? Unfortunately, they're left out in the cold most of the time. They only get sex when their women aren't too tired to give it to them. This, of course, does not fulfill the male fantasy of a virgin princess at his beck and call. Let's look at the reality. In life, there is work, bills, children, housekeeping, taking out the trash, and love. What takes priority? Most of the time, it's work first, children second, bills and housekeeping third, and when there is any time left over, it is for love.

Life's disappointments lead to resistance, resentment, and revenge; the 3 R's as I call them. Women, because of believing in fairy tales, trust that their ideal man, their prince charming, is going to come along on a white horse and rescue them from the daily drudgery. When this doesn't happen, a tiny shred of resistance grows into resentment. As each decade passes, it becomes more apparent that the fairy tale life is a dream, and will never be a reality. That's when resentment grows into revenge. As a result, women get mean to their spouses because the fairy tale isn't true. Then the prince charming is surprised that the princess has grown mean.

Men seem to be oblivious to the reality that life duties and chores must still get done. Who is going to do all the work if one of these two doesn't? Men think they have fulfilled their duties as men if they go to work, make a lot of money, and come home every day. A lot of men will take care of the children, some cook, and a few even clean house and take out the trash. For the most part, however, men think that taking care of the house and family are the woman's responsibilities. Who pays the bills? Probably whoever finds it the least distasteful. On top of all of this is the issue of sex for which neither has time or energy. How can a woman not feel disappointment when her hopes and dreams have been crystallized by a fairy tale and her man remains oblivious?

I know I sound like I am preaching and really heaping criticism on men. In truth, I'm heaping criticism on both men and women. Every day, I hear complaints from married women about their men. They sound something like this:

"I take care of the kids, I do the laundry, dishes, cleaning, shopping, and most of the cooking, plus I have a job, too. He goes to work, hangs out (plays golf, drinks beer, goes to games, or even strip clubs) with business associates, and thinks it's a big deal to watch the kids for a few hours while I do the shopping or go to the gym. When I get home, he wants sex. When do I get a break? I really don't mind that he goes out with the guys. It's just that it would be nice for him to put as much planning into having a night out with me on occasion."

Then there is the other point of view from the men:

"I go to work every day, long hours; I make good money. Then the minute I come home, she wants me to take the kids or go shopping or something. I watch the kids so she can go to the gym and shopping but she is never satisfied. No matter what I do, it doesn't seem to be enough. She is always mad at me and she never wants to have sex anymore."

What's going on here is a lack of clarity, appetite, orders, and appreciation. Women have a part in this process as well. Their expectations of men are rarely met because they haven't been clearly expressed. In addition, women have such high standards for themselves that they are unwilling to let the men do things their way because it won't be good enough.

Primitive drives are at the source of these traditions. If we look back in our history to caveman and early pioneer days, women were the home, hearth, heart, and source of the nurturing, love and togetherness. Men were the ones accountable for bringing home the bacon, so to speak. They also were responsible for defending the home. In those pioneer and caveman days, there was no TV, no computers, no vehicles, and no telephones. So I ask you, what was there to do when everyone was home? The answer is that they would talk and make love.

A source of male domination is physical prowess. Since the man was responsible for the family's survival, (food-wise and protection-wise), he held the power. The woman was responsible for the togetherness, comfort, and nurturing of the family. These were deeply ingrained instincts that are still present in all of us. What goes on currently is that both men and women fight these instincts.

Women want to be recognized for their brains, their creativity, and their ability to cope with the working world as well as being the mother, wife, and homemaker. They really have high expectations of themselves. Men still have their physical prowess. However, it's not needed as much as it used to be. Women can survive without men. Neither however, can survive without love.

Men do what comes naturally and dominate as an act of love. Their domination is currently met with the 3 R's (resistance, resentment, and revenge). What would happen if they just surrendered to the concepts that are instinctual to each gender? I am not suggesting a return to the caveman days, but how about some universal acceptance that men are powerful physical providers, and women are social, nurturing home creators? Perhaps that point of view would remove some of the competition between men and women.

What happens when these truths are rejected is that women get mean and men get bewildered. Men do not know how to behave. They want to please women and instinctively think that dominating and being a man is the way to do it. Women, on the other hand, get resentful because they want to go into the business world and use their brains to display their talents, and yet they are still expected to be the woman of the house. This creates the 3 R's in them and because there is no way out of this dilemma, they get mean.

It is hard to believe but a woman's wrath against a man she loves is actually an act of love. It displays her willingness to express her emotions freely and demonstrates her trust in his love. So now that this scenario is in place, what needs to happen to compensate for all of this and get everyone what we want in the way of relationship? Acknowledgement of these truths and movement towards simplification of the process is a start. Divorce is not. Men want sex, comfort, and approval. Women want freedom, acknowledgement of their intelligence, and sensual satisfaction.

Victims of disillusionment, both men and women end up sacrificing their relationships and their love by leaving the relationship and starting over again only to discover that nothing has changed.

Why Do Relationships End?

Most often a relationship ends because a woman dismisses her man. In some instances, women get so mean that the man chooses to leave rather than live with the wrath. However, most often, it is the woman who ends a relationship. Men don't leave unless they are forced to do so. Oh yes, there are those philandering men who want two twenties for their forty-year-old wife, but most often they would rather keep the forty and just add the two twenties.

A woman will dismiss a man when he has disappointed her in some way, usually when she realizes he's not the man she thought he was. How? By violating a value or crossing some undefined line of belief that the woman holds sacred. Or, he just ignores her enough that she gets disgusted and leaves. It is usually about integrity or honor, or something equally as significant.

It takes a lot of courage to end a long-term commitment, especially when there are children involved, property, money, in-laws, and love. It can take many years of wanting something to change, and attempting to improve the relationship before someone in a long-term relationship will make the move to end the marriage. Usually it is one incident that violates a value that is sacred to the one who ends it, that provokes the last straw.

One of the most difficult things I ever did was to leave my relationship of 23 years; a marriage to a man I dearly loved, but whose actions I could no longer tolerate. I remember that for years I would cry myself to sleep, wishing he would be a jerk so that I could justify leaving him. What I didn't know then was it was my own fault that things had turned out the way they did. I had not assumed my power as a woman in the relationship.

It's interesting that feminine power has more to do with self-esteem than any other issue. A man will produce for a woman. That's instinctual. He will seek her approval and he wants to please her. He needs direction, and if a woman cannot express her appetite and ask for the things she needs, he will not provide them, and she will be disappointed.

This was the reality of my marriage. I never asked for anything. I knew I could do it myself and better than he could. Thus, he quit producing anything for me. He loved me but didn't know how to please me. I loved him and thought I was saving him by not asking for anything. Over time, I began to doubt his production ability and I lost respect for him. Then I dismissed him because he violated his own integrity trying to impress me. We were lost.

As much as I hate to admit it, ending a relationship where there is true love is the easy way out. I recognize that when I did it, I had run out of options and felt that I had tried everything. What I hadn't tried was what I didn't know that I didn't know. That is where you come in. I want you to recognize that two people who love each other can find a way to be together if they really want to. What is the greater truth about that? It's a choice.

What is the most challenging aspect about surviving in a relationship? Nothing. The challenge is in finding a new way of being that will allow space for everything. What could possibly encompass the faults, virtues, gifts, desires, wants, needs, and pleasure of both parties in the relationship? Could it be the desire to be together? What if it is vulnerability? What if the willingness to stop protecting your image, would release the three R's? What if the ability to be exactly who you are with all of your blemishes and mistakes, allows you to still be in love? What if you could love each other's faults? I know this reads like idealistic drivel, but there is a thread of truth and reality here that I am struggling to capture.

"Unconditionally loving someone for who they are has nothing to do with loving someone for what they do." Being together is a choice, and each choice is based on whether both partners are willing to find their own unique path. It will not be the same for everyone. Each person is challenged with different crosses. How they choose to overcome those challenges creates who they are. If men and women could stop mating their idealistic images and start mating their souls instead, it's possible that the divorce rate would decrease. It's possible that life would improve. It's possible that love would be rekindled, along with passion. In the big picture, intimates could be happy and thrive.

The "How to Get What You Want from Your Man Anytime" Strategy

- Be direct.

- Acknowledge him graciously and honestly.

- Use your appetite to ask for EXACTLY what you want.

- Ignore his hesitation and objections.

- Recognize when he violates one of your MAJOR standards and never settle.

- When he produces the result you want, show your appreciation.

- Dismiss him completely when he doesn't produce for you.

Chapter 8
Truth and Denial

"So many people are out of touch with their feelings. When we have suppressed and closed off our feelings, we cannot contact the universe within us, we cannot hear our intuitive voice and we certainly can't enjoy being alive."

—Shakti Gawain, *Living in the Light*

Reality and truth travel a very narrow path. What is the truth? It actually is a perception. There is no proof in the universe that anything is a truth. Many things perceived as truths have been disavowed after more is discovered. So in terms of relationship, where is the line between truth and a lie, or truth and dishonesty? What does it mean to have truth in a relationship?

More and more I discover that truth for one partner is not necessarily the same for the other. So when I say that it is important to tell the truth in a relationship, what it means is that you must tell the truth, as you perceive it to be for you. There is no universal truth about anything. The truth is simply your truth and nothing more. So in explaining a situation to your significant other, what is presented is the truth according to you. As told from several others who witnessed or participated in an incident, the truth could be a totally different picture. The truth involves telling your experience of an incident and giving your interpretation of that event and what it means to you. The key to this concept is that you are completely honest.

Denial is lying to yourself about what really happened. It is an act designed to make you look good to the world. How does it serve you? In some ways, it allows you to delay the response and avoid dealing with some of the repercussions of your situation. In the long run, denial is a place that is harmful to you. In terms of relationship, marriage particularly, denial is at the heart of the "out of control" divorce rate. So many marriages are conducted in denial simply because people are so busy and overwhelmed by life itself that they ignore all the clues that indicate that their marriage is in trouble.

It is only when it becomes a crisis that either partner chooses to address it, and at that time they act like it is a surprise. It is because they have both been lying to themselves about the condition of their relationship. It is the first time that one of them gets hurt, offended, slighted, shocked, or surprised by their partner's behavior or response that intervention is necessary. It is not when they are at their wits end trying to deal with their partner's inattention, abusive behavior, obvious lying, inappropriate actions or even awkward explanation of some event.

It all boils down to not wanting to admit to being wrong about this person. Take this example: Carrie and Joe are engaged. Carrie has placed Joe on a pedestal and endowed him with all of her standards and expectations about his character and integrity. Their plans are going forward until some little incident occurs, i.e., Joe goes to Vegas and loses $2,000 of their money. She loves him and doesn't want to deal with him being less than the person that she has decided that she envisioned. So she makes it okay by ignoring the situation. That is the beginning of the end.

I am not saying that you have to be an anal-retentive obsessive about this, but it's necessary to be aware, be present, and address things as they occur. Think about it the way someone would approach a new job. It takes several months of paying careful attention to details to become competent on your job. When people get married, they instantly think they have rapport and know how to be with each other. The reality is: it takes more than a year to know each other well enough to pick up on the clues. There are no training protocols for marriage, and I don't know that it would be a good idea anyway, but the wedding is only the start of the engagement, not the end.

Secrets and Lies

Past experiences generate fear, which in turn generates the inclination to lie your way out of a situation. It is a pattern learned in childhood, which frequently is never replaced. Have you ever experienced that cold flash of fear that occurs when you think you have made a mistake? Then later you discover that the response was generated by an emotional flashback to some actual incident in the past. Those incidents are referred to as anchors and can be triggered by various signals stored in the subconscious mind. Anchors are too complicated to go into here, but just know that the responses that are generated by these anchors are as real as the original event.

Sleight of hand misleads those who observe. So where does it say that omission or a lie of omission is an avoidance of the truth? What is a lie of omission, anyway? Is it when you forget to tell your significant other something important? I don't think so. The factor that makes something a lie is the intent behind the communication. That is why it is so easy to misinterpret someone's communication. We never really know what someone's intent is unless they make that clear to us in the communication. It is really a wonder that anyone is ever understood.

Communication is an art, a learned skill and takes considerable practice to master it. Things which are forgotten are not lies, unless it was intentional to forget them. So here is where it all gets tricky. Whatever is said can be considered the truth, depending on the intent. Individuals have complete control over their communication; however they have no control over what others perceive to be the truth. For example, if a lie is told with the intent to be truthful, is it a lie?

Intention seems to be the most significant aspect of truth. If deceiving someone is the purpose of your words, it is a lie. If someone is misled by hearing partial truths, statements out of context, or by not receiving important data, it is a lie. Something someone forgot to mention is not a lie, unless the intent was to omit it. So it seems that lying is a conscious act with intent to deceive and harm.

Avoidance of confrontation is one of the major reasons for lies. Ironically this leads to more significant confrontations down the line. It always seems to me that any kind of lie will eventually come back to haunt you. I must have learned that as a child because I've never been a very good liar.

Light shining on any subject creates exposure, and light shining on secrets and lies creates an opening for exponential growth. There is magic in the truth. When I work with married clients, the major part of the work we do revolves around speaking the truth to each other. Through a series of monitored conversations called "withhold sessions," each person is led through a series of incomplete statements, which they complete. Each participant has two minutes to speak on each statement. They are instructed to say everything that comes into their mind that is triggered by the statement.

Sometimes a lot comes pouring out; other times the two minutes are spent in silence. The statements are designed to bring out the true, submerged feelings of each toward the other. This is a communication shift for most married couples, so it is designed to start slowly with simple statements.

As the session progresses, the statements get more intimate and more direct, and the listening participant is only allowed to respond to his/her partner by saying, "thank you." The participants quickly penetrate to deeper levels of their consciousness. It is an exciting and cleansing process and most clients find out things about their partners that they never suspected. Interestingly, they also find out things about themselves that they never suspected. It is very difficult to lie in a session like this, so the truth prevails.

Ignorance Creates Doubt in Relationships

Ignorance about what your partner thinks or feels leads to creating fantasy to fill the gaps. People in relationship tend to create their own interpretations about unexplained events. They think they know each other. Women tend to think they understand men and know what they are thinking, but rarely is this true. The only way to know what someone is thinking is to ask them at the time when you want to know. Men rarely claim to know what women are thinking. They just don't even bother to go there.

I have coined a rather crude phrase in my relationship coaching that goes right to the heart of this issue. When a woman does not know what her man is doing, often she will make up what she thinks he is doing and accuse him of that. For example, early in my coaching career, a woman named Rebecca came to see me. She had a steady boyfriend named Robert, and they were in a committed relationship, but they didn't live together. Rebecca knew that Robert had a former girlfriend named Dorene, and whenever Rebecca needed to see Robert and couldn't find him, she was certain that he was cheating on her with Dorene. When all was said and done and it was determined where he actually had been, she was always wrong. She had simply created this fantasy in her head and it was so real for her that she could justifiably accuse him of cheating behind her back.

This was not an isolated incident subject to her paranoia. This type of reaction occurs with most women when they do not know where their man is. They create a scenario of what they believe is happening and make it true.

They then accuse their partner of the transgression they believe is true. In my practice, I call this a "Doing Dorene" incident. It is a common occurrence. It is one reason that men justifiably do not understand women.

Scenario: Imagination with Paranoia

Adrianna and Eric have been dating for awhile. They are moving into a more serious relationship and have started sleeping together and having sex. They do not live together. Eric calls her to see how her day is going about 2:00 p.m. and tells her that he has to work late.

While they are on the phone, Adrianna can hear voices in the background and Eric interrupts their conversation to respond to something someone in his office has said to him. He's holding his hand over the receiver to muffle the sound. As he resumes their conversation, Adrianna hears female laughter in the background.

This is the conversation taking place in Adrianna's head: "It sounds like they are having fun. Does he really have to work late? Maybe that is just a story so he can go out with his office friends. What did he say to them about me? Who is that woman talking to him? What did he say about me? Why are they laughing at me? How can he lie to me this way?"

By the time Eric hangs up the phone and goes back to work, he has been accused, tried, convicted, and hung. Actually, nothing happened except he called to say he had to work late. Eric's conversation with his co-workers had absolutely nothing to do with Adrianna.

Eric is under the impression that everything is fine with them, while Adrianna is devastated and convinced that Eric is cheating on her. Later that evening about 7:00 p.m., Eric calls Adrianna again to give her an update on when he thinks he will be finished.

Eric

Hi babe, I'm still here and it looks like I'll be at least another hour or two. We just ordered a pizza. Sorry, I know you fixed dinner. I'll make it up to you. (Adrianna is so beside herself with grief that she cannot even answer the phone. Eric has spoken to her answering machine.)

The conversation in Adrianna's head continues: "That's a likely story. He's probably at a bar with that woman. I don't understand how he can lie to me like that. He's only calling me to cover his ass. He thinks if he calls me I won't suspect anything. I wonder how long this has been going on. Who is she?" (Adrianna is broken-hearted and weeping by this time. She is living in her fantasy of what is happening. Eric's cheating is not a suspicion. It has become her reality.)

Eric calls again at 9:00 p.m., and this time, Adrianna answers the phone.

Eric

Hi Ad, I am finally done. I'll be heading over to your place in about five minutes.

Adrianna (Answers coldly)

Don't bother. It's so late, I'm going to bed.

Scenario Analysis

Adrianna will spend the entire night in pain, brooding about how Eric cheated on her. When Eric does see Adrianna again, she will be very angry with him. He will not understand why. From Adrianna's point of view, this is grounds for a breakup unless Eric discovers her suspicions and dispels them.

What actually happened here?

- Eric had to work late

- Eric was being considerate of Adrianna to call and tell her what was going on

- Eric called her three times when he didn't have to call her at all

- Eric obviously cares about her and is thinking of her

- There is no other woman

- Adrianna is consumed with jealousy and insecurity

- Adrianna has no self-esteem

- Adrianna is immersed in her own paranoia.

Speaking Your Truth

Truth is a slippery thing. Everyone comes with baggage and most relationships have some dirty laundry. So much of what I say about having complete honesty in a relationship will be colored by each person's history, and the baggage they carry from their former relationships. It's best to try and clean all of that out of their consciousness, but it still remains in their unconscious. It can't be avoided. The only way to deal with these shadows and ghosts is to expose them.

I don't mean that you should dump your entire history on your partner when you first meet him, but as incidents occur and those anchored emotions surface, enroll your partner in the exploration and exposure of your fears and anxiety. For some this may be a lifelong process, but for most, a few sessions where you bare your soul and your most embarrassing moments will be enough to establish the kind of trust, intimacy, and vulnerability that is necessary for a solid, whole, committed heterosexual relationship.

Most of the time, it is not the present circumstances that are the cause of distress. It is most often some incident in the past where a decision was made that is affecting your life as an adult in your current relationship. Get it out and deal with it. The more shadows you lurk in, the less safe your relationship will be. This is what "tell the truth" means.

Listen for the truth in everything. Congruency validates honesty. It's obvious when watching someone lie, that they are lying. Their body language usually gives them away. Only the most experienced double agents are proficient at congruently lying. Listen for consistency in the overall message. Watch the eyes. Little kids are notorious for announcing their lies. They fidget, roll their eyes, turn color, stammer, and stutter. Do you really think that adults outgrow their inability to hide their lying eyes?

From the reverse perspective, children are great lie detectors. They can tell when an adult is lying to them. They know when their parents are unhappy, angry, cheating, lying or whatever. The unfortunate part of this scenario is that children usually take the blame for everything upon themselves. If a parent is angry, they assume it is something they have done. When divorces occur, the children usually assume that they are at fault.

An emotional lie is a term assigned to the scenario where you lie to children about emotions that are occurring. For example, if a couple has a violent argument and the child walks in, the parents assume a silent posture. When the child asks if everything is okay, the parent lies and says everything is fine. This child knows that everything is not fine, but the parents persist with the lie until the child leaves the room. Then they resume their argument.

Consistently behaving in this way will cause permanent damage in your children. Research this if you don't believe me. It's documented in many books about dysfunction and co-dependence. Typically, teenagers will confront this behavior in their parents, but not always. If you are having an affair and you have teenagers, don't think that you have fooled them. They know.

Scenario: Seduction in Denial

Truth and denial exist all around us. It can be very subtle or blatant. Denial is undetectable until long after you are in it. We've all seen this happen, but how many of us have actually experienced recognizing the denial that takes place in this example of instant attraction to a man in the workplace? It goes like this: one person is the boss, and the other is a subordinate. He is married. She is not. He makes a move and she says no. Let's see what it might look like in the following example.

Joanne

I can't do this with you.

Tom

Why not?

Joanne

Because you're married and you work for me.

Tom

So I have to quit my job and leave my wife to have you?

Joanne

Yes.

They agree he is married, and they shouldn't get together. The attraction remains. They flirt. She continues to say no. He tries harder. He behaves charmingly. He is attentive. He is physically attractive to her. He pursues her. He is seductive. He touches her hand. He looks into her eyes. He is impressed by her intelligence and competence at work.

She tells him he is very attractive and just what she is looking for if only he weren't married. He is turned on because he knows she wants him and yet she is still saying no. He gets even more aggressive and blatant about his flirting.

One day she is slightly vulnerable and agrees to have a drink with him. She still says no to an affair, but they talk about everything. She feels heard and understood. In all actuality, the affair has already started. She is saying no verbally, but yes in her mind. He is challenged because he knows she wants him and the chase is on.

They continue to flirt secretly. They believe that no one has noticed their attraction to one another. Something dramatic happens to one of them, usually her. She gets fired because of him is a likely scenario. She is vulnerable and she finally gives in.

Three months into the sexual affair, they have the following discussion:

Joanne

You are the best thing that has ever happened to me. I love you so much. I want you to leave your wife and come live with me (or marry me).

Tom

That will never happen.

Joanne

Why?

Tom

Because I am married and I love my wife.

Scenario Analysis

What happened here? She is shocked that he said no. He has broken her heart. One of two things occurs next. Either she accepts his answer and stops the affair, or she settles for being the other woman, convinced that he will change his mind because their love is so powerful. Relationships like this have been known to go on for decades. She was in denial when she initially said no. He was in denial about his marriage, his love for his wife and his ability to keep love and sex separate. His seduction was a lie. He may have been feeling the attraction but he never had any intention of being in a relationship. It was a game of seduction to him.

Lying Conveys Many Messages

Living a lie, staying in a marriage that isn't working, or not separating for the sake of the children, are just a few of the more common, compounded lies. What is happening when someone remains in a loveless relationship teaches children that the truth doesn't matter. It teaches them relationship integrity doesn't matter. It teaches them that sacred intimacy is a farce. It teaches them to cheat. It perpetuates the demise of the sanctity in marriage for future generations.

So don't fool yourself that you are doing the honorable thing to stay in a marriage that is destructive for the sake of the children. When you do, you are not just lying to yourself, you are lying to your partner and lying to your children and teaching them to disrespect the opposite sex. You are living in denial.

Silence is the ultimate lie. Withholding communication is for me the most difficult of all lies. When a partner shuts down and stubbornly refuses to participate on any level, it leaves you with nothing of substance.

I remember that my husband would use silence as a means of punishing me when he was angry with me for something. It drove me to the brink of violent behavior more than anything else he ever did. I would go to extremes to provoke any kind of response from him. The more silent he got, the more outrageous I got. It didn't work for either one of us. I got crazier and he just got more silent. There is no space in relationship for silence. Relationship is based on communication and trust.

◆ ◆ ◆

The "How to Get What You Want from Your Man Anytime" Strategy

- Be direct.

- Acknowledge him graciously and honestly.

- Use your appetite to ask for EXACTLY what you want.

- Ignore his hesitation and objections.

- Recognize when he violates one of your MAJOR standards and never settle.

- When he produces the result you want, show your appreciation.

- Dismiss him completely when he doesn't produce for you.

Chapter 9
Don't Settle—Renovate

"Your relationship doesn't have to be in trouble. You do not have to become one more fatality in the runaway epidemic of broken hearts. You can reach out and reconnect with your partner, and build a memorable life together. But the deck is stacked against you unless you start dealing right now with the truth about you and the life you and your partner have created together."
—Dr. Philip C. McGraw, *Relationship Rescue*

Good sex means a good relationship. Not always, but most of the time. Sex can be used as a weapon and withholding sex can be a means of punishment between partners. What I am saying is that sex is a barometer for the health of a relationship. When a man and a woman have a healthy sex life and are attracted to each other, it is a measure of how much intimacy they share. Of course, there are exceptions to this rule in that some people simply have hot, passionate, non-intimate sex, but those are not the people to whom I am referring. I am talking about people who are married to each other or who are living in a committed relationship and who talk to each other. They have comfortable, playful, intimate sex two to three times a week. Sex on those terms creates an opening to intimacy that is not achieved by any other means of communication.

Desire for sex, which is rejected by a partner, can be a characteristic of withheld anger, frustration, and revenge. Eleven of the thirteen characteristics of sexual turn-on are present in anger. Yet righteous anger can be a significant impediment to sexual intimacy. Anger that is unexpressed and suppressed can return as sexual impassivity or resistance to romance. Everyone knows that when you are truly hurt and angry, it is difficult to feel loving and sexual. Some people, however, recognize that anger is a turn-on and they fight just for the purpose of making up because the sex is that much better when emotions are high. Anger that is unexpressed and stuffed deep inside you will return to impede intimacy.

Dealing with a Highly Emotional Partner

Silence is a powerful means of expressing anger and one of men's favorite methods of withholding their emotional honesty. Coldness and unresponsiveness can lead to violence from a partner who is highly emotional. It is immensely frustrating to be angry and want to express that anger and get to the bottom of an issue when the person to whom it's directed is cold and withdrawn. Typically it is men who respond that way and most women will go crazy to get any type of a response from the stoic unresponsive male.

Women, being the "emotional sort" that they are, have a tendency to get outrageous in their attempts to elicit a response from the man who shuts down communication during a disagreement. Men tend to withdraw from conflict with their women. Whether this is because they fear their own violence in responding with real anger or whether they just can't tolerate confrontation. Such passive-aggressive behavior does nothing to support an intimate relationship. In return, violent, out-of-control anger doesn't support intimacy either and it rarely elicits any kind of response from the man who uses silence as a weapon. So this routine doesn't work for either party. Those who play this game do so out of habit, not because it brings about any resolution of their differences.

Unsatisfied needs, ignored requests, and simple frustrations are the leading motivators for the concept known as nagging. It is only when a request has not been honored that the requesting spouse feels the need to nag. Even though nagging has been unquestionably proven to fail at getting results, it still remains the method of choice for unfulfilled requests with most women.

Nagging has been the source of amusement for family-oriented sit-coms since the beginning of television. Throughout many generations, mothers have taught daughters, and fathers have taught sons how to respond to each other. What has been taught on TV has people actually behaving so automatically that no one thinks to question the process.

Psychologists call it positive reinforcement. Marriage counselors call it manipulation. I call it a strategy that works. The best way to get anyone to respond to your request is to acknowledge that person for something they have actually done right, and then present your request in a clear, straightforward manner. Making a request of someone is like ordering from a menu. You order, and then acknowledge and appreciate any movement in the direction of accomplishment. It works every time. Why we forget this is the ultimate question.

Understanding Disapproval and Confrontations

Disapproval creates distance between partners. Denial of wrongdoing becomes a way of life. Snide comments create pain and separation, and yet this is what most people resort to when they become frustrated. Direct confrontation is rarely anyone's choice for getting through the three R's (resistance, resentment, and revenge) that are triggered by snide comments, unresponsiveness, and downright angry responses.

How do people who love each other arrive at these diametrically opposed stances where no one wins? The first and most significant reason is that they forget that when they are committed to each other, they are and will always be on the same side. They forget that they have decided to be a team united against any assault from the entire universe. Perhaps some of their forgetfulness arises from the inherent anger that women possess. Or, perhaps it is perpetuated by their instinctive, aggressive, confrontational, and violent physical responses. Since men know that they cannot respond to women with violence, their next best choice is to be snide, hostile, and withdrawn. Thus, the cycle begins and leads to loss of intimacy, alienation between the sexes, and the ultimate deterioration of love and marriage.

Avoidance of confrontation can be an excuse not to go home. Using work as an excuse to avoid your spouse's neediness becomes another way of avoiding intimacy. A tired man heading home to a tired wife who is also heading home to three needy, neglected children can be fertile fields for lack of intimacy and avoidance of sex.

The Danger of Assuming a Conclusion

Just because communication is assumed to be clear does not validate that it is. Often times, by asking the simple question, "What did you mean by that?" without anger or agenda can result in an explanation that takes the conversation in an entirely different direction. Reaction is often the trigger to an argument when instead, taking a breath; pausing and asking for the meaning can result in entirely more pleasant outcomes.

Major issues can create irreconcilable differences when they arise in the context of a relationship. It is frequent that lovers assume that because they are alike in so many ways that they will agree on everything important that arises in their lives. This could not be further from the truth. Everyone has formed their own ideas from personal experiences, history, genetics, and family dynamics that can surface and create major dissension. If these things can be discussed and decided prior to marriage, they can prevent a lot of heartache later.

Neglect, lack of approval and varying levels of sexual needs are incendiary issues that can lead to infidelity. Even though practically everyone is tempted to stray, what is it that binds people to their vows? It is a choice that one makes to be faithful to a partner. When you marry someone for love and make that commitment to fidelity, it need not be a prison sentence.

If you are in a relationship where the two of you are in love, approve of each other, and are committed to building a life together, cheating would not be possible as long as you are honest and vulnerable with each other. When you have the kind of love, respect and passion for each other that can be generated in a relationship of integrity, the thought of another man or woman would not even occur to you. That does not mean that you would not necessarily be attracted to someone else. It just means that you wouldn't go there because the honor between you and your partner is so strong that you could not violate that sacred trust. This kind of bond takes attention and continual reaffirmation, and a lot of sexual intimacy.

Settling for less than what you want, the absence of clear boundaries, and the unwillingness to sacrifice comfort for integrity are all issues which create compromise in relationships. Making a bad deal in a marriage can result in years of serving sentences, which are tantamount to imprisonment. An example would be the man who gives up his dream of starting his own business, because his wife does not support his willingness to take the risk and giving up a guaranteed salary in his 9-5 accounting job.

Another example is a wife who is quite miserable with her philandering and inattentive husband who stays in the marriage because she has financial security for herself and her children.

How about the woman who bypasses her childbearing years in a career only to discover that she waited too long and now is unable to conceive and bear children? Selling out your integrity for comfort is frequently the deal that people make in order to live their lives without risk and confrontation.

Understanding Acceptance and Denial

After a couple has an argument over a trust issue in the relationship, what frequently occurs is acceptance and denial because it will keep the family unit together. The non-guilty party accepts that the incident didn't mean anything. The situation is never completely discussed, cleansed, purged, or forgiven.

What you will see in most situations is a neat packaging of the incident so it can be stored away. Then staged forgiveness occurs with the package lurking in the background like a guillotine for the next time the guilty party makes a mistake of any kind. Reparation by the transgressor can never be made. It's a type of emotional blackmail that serves to further alienate the two parties concerned.

Damage can be controlled and reversed after a serious break in trust, but it takes a huge effort by both parties to reevaluate and explore what happened. Then both parties must make effective changes in behavior to rebuild the integrity, intimacy, and love that has been destroyed. You notice I said both parties. That means that both the man and the woman are equally responsible for the transgression. There are no innocent parties when trust is broken. On some level, the "innocent victim" has contributed to his/her partner's motives in their transgression. These contributing behaviors need to be explored and changed or the underlying cause will remain and it will occur again. It is a type of enabling.

Scenario: An Issue of Trust

Here is an example of a sincere attempt to rebuild a relationship after a major violation of integrity and values. Let's see how it turns out:

Rick and Lisa were dating when Rick's ex-girlfriend announced that she was pregnant with Rick's child. Lisa stood by while Rick dealt with the pregnancy and Lilia's intention to have the child.

It resulted in several weeks of drama, arguments, and decision-making, but Lisa waited, content in the knowledge that Rick was the man for her and proud of him for his taking responsibility for his irresponsible actions. Finally, the situation was resolved and Lisa and Rick could resume their relationship. For a year they dated, and then they broke up again because Lisa wanted to get married and Rick insisted that he was not ready for marriage or children.

Several months later, Rick met Lisa again and realized that he really loved her and perhaps it was time for him to grow up and assume some responsibility. Let's see what happened next.

Rick

Lisa, I was so wrong. You are the woman for me. I am ready to settle down and have a family and I want you to be the mother of my children.

Lisa

Rick, you are the man that I have always felt was most compatible with me. I was attracted to you from the moment we met. I have always loved you but you were so irresponsible. I want you to prove to me that you are responsible and sincere about this. I won't consent to marry you until I am sure that you are a changed man who is serious about commitment and marriage.

So they began seeing each other again and had progressed to living together when Rachel, another of Rick's ex-girlfriends called and informed him that she was pregnant with his child and would be having the baby. This is the conversation that followed.

Rick (on the phone with Rachel)

Hi Rachel, how are you?

Rachel

Don't ask me how I am. I am three months pregnant with your child and I want to have this baby.

Rick

What?

Rachel

You heard me. I am pregnant and we are going to have a baby.

Rick

But we broke up and I am back with Lisa and how do I know that it's my child?

Rachel

Because I said so. I haven't been with anyone except you for the past six months and I want to have this baby. So you are going to marry me.

Rick

No. No, this can't be true. I don't want a child with you.

Rachel

You had better reconsider because I am having this baby with or without you and you will still be the father of my child. So you had better come over here and discuss what we are going to do with my parents.

Rick

Okay I'll come over and talk.

Later that evening, Lisa arrives home and is happy to see Rick but she notices that he looks distressed.

Lisa

Hi Honey, I'm home. How was your day?

Rick

You aren't going to believe what happened today!

Lisa

Try me.

Rick

I don't know how to tell you this.

Lisa

Just tell me. We know each other too well for games.

Rick

Remember that girl Rachel that I was seeing while we were separated?

Lisa

Sure, you said she was a spoiled only child of very wealthy indulgent parents.

Rick

Well, she called me today.

Lisa

What did she want?

Rick

She said she is pregnant and it's my child.

Lisa gets very pale and starts shaking.

Lisa

Oh no. Not again. Rick, I can't and won't go through this again. How could you?

Rick

I'm not sure it's even my child.

Lisa

How can you say that?

Rick

Well she could have been with someone else.

Lisa

You told me that you hadn't slept with her. How could you have lied to me like that?

Rick

I knew you would be upset.

Lisa

Upset? I am not upset. I am finished. This is never going to work with us. I could never trust that you were not screwing someone else. I won't live that way. Good-bye, Rick.

Scenario Analysis

Lisa was a slow learner. It took two episodes of being hit by a two-by-four for her to realize that Rick was a philanderer and would never change. He was careless and reckless with his sexual encounters and though Lisa wanted to believe that he would be different with her, she finally recognized that this was not the case. It was a hard lesson for her, but Lisa did not settle. Lisa dismissed Rick and wished him well. Rick convinced Rachel to have an abortion, just as he did with Lilia. Whether or not Rick learned from his multiple experiences is yet to be proven.

Honoring a Sacred Promise

A sacred promise is the commitment in marriage. Sacred means honored, venerable, and holy. Promise means your word, your integrity, and putting your life on the line. Commitment is a scary word that means your ass is on the line. So with all of these heavy words tied to marriage, it is no wonder that people hesitate.

What if a sacred promise was a vow to yourself to hold this person above all else in the world? To honor this person with your innermost thoughts, desires, mistakes, faults, and accomplishments, and that this person honored you the same way. What if marriage wasn't about paying bills, raising kids, competing with the Jones's nor having a better job? What if it was personal, sacred and simply a vow between two people to cherish each other as best friends and lovers with holy honesty forever? What if that is all that marriage is?

Prioritizing needs, delivering withholds, valuing what is most important in another person, these are the things necessary to sustain a marriage. If a marriage was consummated for the right reasons, those being love, honor, integrity and wanting to be together, that marriage can be saved if both parties are willing to return to those basic values and begin again.

Honesty during withholds, delivering all undelivered communication, and recognizing that the purpose of relationship is to heal old wounds can all contribute to the restoration and revitalization of a marriage that has strayed from mutual satisfaction.

If sex is on the rocks and withholds can be delivered non-judgmentally and with utter honesty, the damage can be halted, the scars and baggage can be cleaned up, and with a bit of consistent preventative management, intimacy, trust and sexual satisfaction can be restored. It is revealing to observe people who love each other relieve each other of baggage that has infiltrated their intimacy and weighed them down with anger and resentment. Through the process of honesty and delivering withholds, it is almost possible to visibly observe sexual attraction returning. Whether they complete the process and maintain the cleanliness of their relationship depends on their willingness. There is only one element required, and that is that both parties want to preserve their love.

The "How to Get What You Want from Your Man Anytime" Strategy

- Be direct.

- Acknowledge him graciously and honestly.

- Use your appetite to ask for EXACTLY what you want.

- Ignore his hesitation and objections.

- Recognize when he violates one of your MAJOR standards and never settle.

- When he produces the result you want, show your appreciation.

- Dismiss him completely when he doesn't produce for you.

Chapter 10

The Winning Formula for Getting What You Want from Your Man Anytime

"The great end is pleasure, which unlike power is truly an end, an experience that is not simply a step to a further end. It includes all the values we presently entertain; it excludes nothing."

—Marilyn French, *Beyond Power*

So now you are independent, stable, and healthy, and you're ready for commitment and that relationship that you have always been awaiting. The question is: "Are you really ready for commitment?"

Are you ready to say, "I forsake all others for you," and mean it? I believe in love and marriage as the ultimate in relationship. That's not to say that everyone who is in a committed relationship has to get married, but the commitment is exactly the same. Love and relationship is the foundation for your life.

Men and women can do anything if they have a system in place to support and nurture them. They can go out into the hard cruel world and get beaten up and abused, taken advantage of, yelled at, cursed at, fight traffic battles and bureaucracy all day, as long as there is somewhere to rejuvenate and someone who believes in them. A good relationship can provide the rock solid foundation to do just that. The commitment is a personal vow, made by each person to be together. When there is a bond that strong between two people, they really can endure and conquer any challenge.

Adults are secure, confident, and free to make any choices that they want in order to further their career, life, and their future the way that they want it. Seeking this kind of relationship requires a whole person searching for another whole person, to bond with, and with the goal to create an entity that is bigger, stronger, and separate from you as individuals. That structure is a relationship, which will be treated as a separate entity.

Choosing to participate in events and projects while taking your own needs, your significant other's needs and your relationship's needs into consideration with each and every decision is essential for having a successful relationship. You are now approaching life as an adult and you can expect to receive the benefits of an adult relationship.

Love, support, acknowledgement, passion, sex, security, fun, excitement, and nurturing are the minimums that you can expect from your relationship once you learn to have an appetite, ask for what you want, and are not willing to settle until you get it. It won't be perfect but the necessary components for perfection exist if you have chosen well and you accept your feminine power and utilize it.

Intuition, creativity, and circular thinking are the qualities that women consistently exhibit which are useful in utilizing feminine power. Women do have the power in relationship. Let's face it, men have the power everywhere else in the world, so if relationship is the foundation of life, let's let them have all the rest and just claim our inherent power as women and use it to make the world a better place. Men really are not that concerned with having power in their relationships. It is the one place that they can be convinced to surrender their power as long as they are receiving some benefit. The benefits they most desire are sex and approval, and in that order. If you are smart, you will find a way to give them what they want, and in return get everything that you want.

Woman power has long tentacles that reach into many avenues of male power in subtle and significant ways. When a man is content with his relationship and his woman is his confidant and champion and he hers, they are an unbeatable team. Many women have brought about remarkable changes in the world with their requests to men. How do we know that Gorbachev's wife didn't influence his actions in resolving animosity between Russia and the U.S? We don't. Since women have the power in relationships, why not take it and use it to everyone's benefit? If a woman uses her feminine power in every aspect of her life, she can get everything she wants, without exception.

Ladies, stop competing with men. Let them win at everything. Acknowledge their power in the world. Give them their masculinity. Ask for what you want and expect to get it without fail. Then appreciate all efforts that are exerted for fulfilling your every desire.

There are men out there who are dysfunctional when relating to women. These are the misogynists, the physical and emotional abusers, the rapists, and murderers. One primary goal when searching for a man is to eliminate all of the above from the contenders.

A real man wants to please his woman. This is a constant. He wants her to be proud of him, approve of him, and believe in him. If a woman can accomplish these things while asking for what she wants, he will always do whatever it takes to "win" for her.

So women, if you want a man to please you, look for one who will produce results for you that you can be proud of, approve of, and believe in. When you find one, you will have the secret to how to get what you want from **your man** anytime. The right man is the secret. Once you find the right one, treat him like a precious discovery. Love him, sex him, empower him, and you will not be disappointed.

The Key Ingredient is Appetite

Appetite is a woman's biggest challenge. I have spoken about appetite throughout this entire book, but what actually is it? What are the elements that comprise a healthy appetite in this sense? First in importance is clarity about what you really want. Second is a method of expressing it. Anyone can start demanding tangible items and more attention, but only those women who practice can learn to deliver an acknowledgement and an order in the same breath. Third is the response. When a man brings you something you have asked for and it isn't anything close to what you really wanted, don't throw it in his face. Acknowledge him for the effort, then correct the order and be appreciative of whatever he brought. He will get better at delivering as you get better at ordering.

Finally, let go of your meanness. Just give it up. If you practice having appetite with everyone, including the trash man and the carry-out boy at the grocery store, at some point down the road you will notice that your meanness has disappeared and you have become gracious, charming, and very attractive all the time.

I know many of you are asking, "Why do I have to do all the changing? Why can't the men change?" The reason is because it isn't the men who are so unhappy with their relationships. Men are content to listen to bitchiness, and are willing to be reamed as long as they know you will still be there. They go for comfort while you want perfection.

There's a story that I heard from Jack Rafferty in his man-woman course that I've told in my teleclasses. One man, in fact, came to my teleclass repeatedly because he loved this story so much.

A woman was practicing her appetite, and one evening she sat next to her husband on the couch.

"Honey, you have been working so hard and the business is just booming. I am so proud of you. You have just done an amazing job of getting new clients. I think I'd like to take you on a trip and if we are going on a trip we need a new car. I want you to buy me a new red Mercedes convertible so we can go."

The next day her husband pulls up in a really fancy, shiny red crew cab pick-up truck with a sun roof. He blindfolds her and takes her out to the truck. When he takes off her blindfold in the front seat of the truck, this is what happens.

"Ooooh! Honey, this truck is beautiful. It's big and it has leather upholstery and even a sun roof. Thank you so much. I love it."

She starts kissing him and loving him and ends up giving him a BJ in the front seat of the truck.

Then she says, "Honey, I really love the truck but I really, really want a Mercedes convertible."

The next day she had her Mercedes.

The gentleman, who loved this story, explained it this way:

"All I could think of was how fast can I get her that car because if buying her a red truck got me a BJ, just imagine what will happen when I get her the Mercedes."

I can't tell you how many times I have witnessed women ask for something, have their man bring them something entirely different and just get ripped up one side and down the other about how stupid he is and that he can't get anything right. Trust me. That method doesn't work. Appetite works. Just accept that there is an element of resentment buried deeply inside of you and decide to give it up before it surfaces. Let men receive their favor and privileges. What does it matter if you are getting what you want? Stop competing with men. Adore them, acknowledge them, and appreciate them for the brave, daring, sexy, masculine creatures that they are and work on your own feminine power.

The part of appetite that creates grief for many women is the actual identification of what they want and then saying the words "I want." There is something little girls learn about being unselfish that really intimidates a lot of women. So practice. Practice every day with everyone. Practice on your kids, on the mailman, on the bank tellers, the gas station attendants, your boss, and the people who work for you. Just practice, and one day you will notice that you don't even have to think about it. It has just become the way you are.

About Men

I feel the necessity to emphasize that this strategy about appetite works for men as well as for women. Indeed, it was a man who introduced me to many of the concepts. When I speak about appetite, it is essential for both men and women to realize that it is not just about tangible items. I am not recommending that women become gold diggers. The idea of appetite is based on win-win concepts. If a man and a woman are committed to each other, they share thoughts and dreams. A woman's appetite will include her man's dreams. If they are on the same side, and have chemistry, love, and compatibility in their relationship, her appetite will reflect their communal goals.

When it comes to the level of relationship requiring comfort zone expansion, it means men must grow their dreams as well. Although women do the steering, men provide the map. Appetite for women includes approval, acknowledgement, and appreciation of the man who provides the production. Production for men includes accomplishment, achievement, and advantages greater than their expectations. Success, contentment, and financial rewards for both will follow. Finally, and this could be the subject for another book, men must remember to approve of their women and shower them with love and affection. Then, the ultimate outcome is that both men and women get what they want from each other.

It's All About Your Self-Esteem

After you have been practicing your appetite for a few years with a man who loves you totally and produces everything for you, you will hit another block. It will sound something like this: I have everything I want and don't know what else I want.

This actually does happen. I have former clients who only call me for help when their appetite gets overwhelmed. What happens at that point is they have to grow and play a bigger game. Go to another level of intimacy, sex, wealth, status, or pleasure; whatever it is that they can imagine. Honestly, this is where it gets really tough for a lot of women.

The key to all of this is having the self-esteem to always ask for what you want, and make it be more than he thinks he can produce, and constantly strive to expand your own comfort zone in the area of appetite. Remember to lavish appreciation on the man who is giving you exactly what you want.

Remember Gina who dumped Craig in the parking lot in Chapter 6? Well, after she met and fell for a pirate who completely demolished her comfort zone and expanded her vision, she was able to find her man. She was finally able to see him when he had been right there all the time. She married a high school acquaintance of hers about ten years ago who has produced for her in a remarkable way. They have two sons and live at the beach. She no longer works and the only time she calls for help is when she realizes that she has run out of appetite and isn't taking extraordinary care of herself.

Straight talk, honesty, and vulnerability are all secondary challenges for both men and women. Say what you mean and mean what you say. Tell the truth to the best of your ability and most of all trust this person that you love with every ounce of vulnerability that you can muster. If both of you can commit to surrender in these few areas, you will experience satisfaction in your loving, intimate relationship beyond what you can imagine.

Pay attention! Stop the deceit with the first little incident. Just don't go there. I promise you that if you can maintain this level of honesty in your relationship, you can have satisfaction. That is a big promise but without fail, I have witnessed relationships go both ways simply because they let their awareness stray in this regard. Attention to detail and awareness of surroundings, feelings, intuition, and inklings will garner the most valuable rewards in loving intimate relationships.

Here is absolutely the most crucial part of the entire message. If you haven't done your homework and picked the right man, you will not get what you want. If by some chance you have married or entered into a relationship with a man who does not produce for you, you cannot change him. It will be necessary to dismiss him. Then, walk up to the highest open balcony that you can find and yell with your loudest, fullest voice, "NEXT!"

I am aware that you may not want to hear that, but if you have done the things described in this book to restore your self-esteem and release your meanness and develop your appetite and your man still does not respond, then he doesn't deserve to have you, and you should start looking for a man who recognizes your power and loves you totally. A man who is equal or better is out there for you.

Use your energy, thoughts, and words to bring potential to the attraction in your relationship. One does not become blind when in a relationship. You will meet people to whom you are attracted for one reason or another. This does not need to detract from your primary relationship. Use that attraction to stimulate your own passion about life and your partner.

We all have hormones and many things will stimulate them on occasion, including working out at the gym because that causes increases in testosterone for both men and women. Use it as a catalyst with your lovemaking. There will always be choices when your commitment is challenged. If your commitment is solid and you are devoted to the preservation of your relationship as a separate entity, the choices will be easy and effortless. For the most part, you will not even notice that a challenge exists. If you doubt your commitment and waver in your vulnerability, it will become difficult and truly challenging. This is certainly one instance in which 100% is easy and 99% is a bitch.

Appreciating Sex

It is imperative to ignore the sexual trivia that is flashed in front of us from every source of stimuli and also mandatory to explore personal limits, religious beliefs and nationally imposed inhibitions about sex in order to expand comfort zones concerning sexual intimacy. Sex is good. Sex was created by God to be pleasurable between men and women. Learn to appreciate the obscure resources that will surface with sustained and progressively intimate sexual vulnerability.

If a woman is satisfied sexually, she will certainly not be mean. Besides, men love sex almost more than anything. Though they don't know what women want, women always know they can make their man happy with sex. A friend of mine's husband wanted to know if I was going to write a book called, "What men want from women," and I said sure, but it would be a really short book consisting of just one page with big letters spelling SEX. He laughed but he didn't deny it. So whatever you do, married or not, find the time for sex and intimacy in your busy life. It will contribute so much to keeping your relationship happy.

So here we are, near the end of this entire strategy on what makes relationship work in this world of chaos, demands, and commitments. There are a few more elements that are necessary to consider in this complex equation. One is that life and relationships move forward whether we want them to or not. We can't ever go back to the way things were, nor can we go back to not knowing anything that we have learned. That sometimes is very irritating, isn't it? I can think of many times when I wanted to not know something because now that I know it, I have to do something about it. Damn!!!

Love is a Changing and Living Process

Love has a funny way of becoming a living process, forever growing, changing, and becoming more complex. Sometimes people grow in different directions at a faster or slower pace, and all of their senses and virtues are called upon to keep up with the sometimes-tumultuous growth. I believe that relationships never end; they merely change.

The second thing of importance to remember is that men and women are different. They have different needs, wants, ways of expressing themselves, thinking, and resolving issues. Their approaches are different, and ultimately it serves us that they are different entities. The bottom line here is that they accept each other's differences and learn to approve of each other rather than trying to change each other. Why not try using these simple principles and see if it produces different results?

The third and most crucial element for women is recognizing that they have the power in relationship. All that is necessary for them to get satisfaction from the men in their lives is to assume their feminine power and nurture their self-esteem to the level that they can define their wants. Then they can stretch the expression of their appetite above and beyond their comfort zones. Expect that a man will produce those results because he wants to please you and for no other reason.

I know it sounds easy on paper and seems harder when you are doing it, but with a little help from a coach or like-minded friends, you can create a support group that keeps you focused and on track. It is possible to turn almost any relationship around if you have the combination of love, chemistry, and compatibility which is necessary for a passionate and committed relationship. Finally, if you are one of those who have some clean-up work to do prior to experimenting with this simple process of approval, expression of your appetite and appreciation for the production that your man provides, you now have the tools to begin your work.

Relationship Check List for the Single Person

If you are single, here's a little check list to see if you are ready for a new relationship:

1. Desire. You must really want to be in a relationship.

2. Self-esteem. Know that you are attractive and have something to offer another person.

3. Financial stability. You should have at least enough income to take care of your housing, basic needs, and have minimal credit card debt.

4. Work. You should have a job that satisfies some of your achievement needs.

5. Vulnerability. By having gone through enough self-healing, you are able to share your authentic self with another person.

6. Love. Above all, you should have an abundance of love for yourself with enough left over to share with another person.

If you have checked off all items in this list, then you are ready to start exhibiting your appetite on those 40 men you need to meet.

I am not saying that you must be in perfect shape. However, you will want to attract a person who is your balance; someone who has the same or similar issues in the same proportions.

If you are needy, you will attract neediness. If you have intimacy issues, you will attract someone who is shut down. So it is in your best interests to undertake a personal re-development plan prior to looking for a relationship.

Be the best you can be, so that you can offer yourself and your love to another person. Funny, how it usually happens that someone who has been taking extraordinary care of themselves and not looking for a relationship, suddenly finds him/herself in love.

Relationship Spring-Cleaning for Couples

If you are married, or in a committed relationship and bogged down, here is where you start:

1. Reserve a weekend where the two of you can be alone and undisturbed for 48 hours.

2. You can do this alone or engage a coach to guide you.

3. Each of you should take along a notebook listing your wants, which will be yours to share or not.

4. Take time to write extensive endings to the following statements:

    a. I am with you because . . .

    b. My feelings were hurt when . . .

    c. I get angry when . . .

    d. I resist new ideas from you when . . .

    e. I resent you when . . .

    f. I want to take revenge on you when . . .

    g. I hate you when . . .

    h. You always . . .

    i. You never . . .

    j. I don't want to forgive you when . . .

    k. I want to believe . . .

    l. I love you because . . .

1. You get the idea. You can add statements that are specific for you as long as they are not accusations and they express your feelings about the situation and your relationship. The goal is to get to the tiniest resentments and hurts that you have stored up for however long you two have been together.

2. Obviously, if you have been married for a long time and have never done anything like this, it might be difficult to get every little thing the first time through, and you may have to repeat this more than once or get someone to guide you through the process.

3. Once you have completed your writing, you are going to share the contents of your writing with your partner.

4. The rules for sharing are as follows:

    a. Only one of you may speak at a time.

    b. The person sharing cannot elaborate.

    c. The person listening cannot comment except to say thank you.

    d. Once you have shared all of this information, release it, and completely let go of your feelings about all of it.

1. The outcome which is desired by completing this process is cleansing and release.

2. The next part of the process involves revitalizing and restoring your passion.

3. Take time to write extensive endings to the following statements:

    a. I forgive you completely for . . .

    b. I appreciate your . . .

    c. I thank you for . . .

    d. I want you to . . .

    e. You turn me on when . . .

    f. I get excited about . . .

    g. I acknowledge your . . .

    h. I am proud of you because . . .

    i. I cherish you for . . .

    j. I love you because . . .

    k. I want to be with you because . . .

1. Repeat steps 5, 6, 7, and 8.

2. The outcome which is desired by this process is attraction and revitalization of your love.

Note: When you are done with this exercise, if you aren't turned on, ready to make love, or don't feel like you just met and fell in love, you haven't cleaned under all the furniture, and you would benefit from more of the same.

So to get what you want from your man anytime, make sure you have the right man, and then do your job. Your number one responsibility in a man-woman relationship is to provide appetite and a direction for the relationship. The only way to accomplish this is to assume your feminine power. If you have gotten this far in reading my book, I hope your comfort zone has been expanded, and your appetite has been stimulated. Nevertheless, you can't ever go back to not knowing all of this.

So go out there and practice. Then maybe one day you'll write or call me with the news that you've found your ideal man who produces the results that you have asked for, and you love every minute of your new life.

Bibliography

Alcoholics Anonymous, *Alcoholics Anonymous*, Alcoholics Anonymous World Services, Inc.: New York City, 1976.

Alessandra, Tony, Ph.D., Wexler, Phil & Barrera, Rick, *Non-Manipulative Selling*, Prentice Hall Press: New York, 1987.

Bach, Richard, *Illusions: The Adventures of a Reluctant Messiah*, Dell Publishing, New York, 1977.

Bandler, Richard and Grinder, John, *Frogs Into Princes*, Real People Press: Moab, 1979.

Beattie, Melody, *Beyond CoDependency and Getting Better All the Time*, A Harper Hazelden Book, Harper & Row, Publishers: San Francisco, 1989.

Brown, Gabrielle, Ph.D., *The New Celibacy: A Journey to Love, Intimacy, and Good Health in a New Age*, McGraw-Hill Publishing Company: New York, 1989.

Buscaglia, Leo, *Loving Each Other: The Challenge of Human Relationships*, Slack, Inc.: Thorofare, 1984.

Chia, Montak and Abroms, Douglas, *The Multi-Orgasmic Man: Sexual Secrets Every Man Should* Know, Harper: San Francisco, 1997.

Cialdini, Robert B., Ph.D., *Influence: How and Why People Agree to Things*, Quill: New York, 1984.

DeAngelis, Barbara, Ph.D., *Are You the One for Me? Knowing Who's Right and Avoiding Who's Wrong*, Dell Publishing: New York, 1992.

_____. *How to Make Love All the Time*, Dell Publishing: New York, 1987.

_____. *Secrets About Men Every Woman Should Know*, Dell Publishing: New York, 1990.

_____. *Make Love Last a Lifetime*, Dell Publishing: New York, 1987.

Eisler, Riane, *The Chalice and the Blade*, Harper & Row Publishers: New York, 1988.

Fein, Ellen and Schneider, Sherrie, *The Rules: Time Tested Secrets for Capturing the Heart of Mr. Right*, Warner Books: New York, 1996.

Forward, Dr. Susan and Torres, Joan, *Men Who Hate Women & The Women Who Love Them*, Bantam Books: New York, 1986.

French, Marilyn, *Beyond Power on Women, Men, and Morals*, Ballantine Books: New York, 1985.

Gawain, Shakti, with King, Laurel, *Living in the Light: A Guide to Personal and Planetary Transformation*, Nataraj Publishing: Novato, 1986.

Gerber, Michael E., *The E Myth: Why Most Businesses Don't Work and What To Do About It*, Ballinger Publishing Company: Cambridge, 1986.

Grant, Susannah, *Erin Brockovich, The Shooting* Script, New Market Press: New York, 2000.

Greer, Germaine, *The Whole Woman*, Alfred A. Knopf, Inc.: New York, 1999.

Hay, Louise L., *You Can Heal Your Life*, Hay House: Santa Monica, 1984.

Helgesen, Sally, *The Female Advantage: Women's Ways of Leadership*, Doubleday: New York, 1990.

Joannides, Paul, *The Guide to Getting It On! The New and Mostly Wonderful Book About Sex for Adults of All Ages*, Goofy Foot Press: Waldport, 1996.

Jong, Erica, *Fear of Fifty*, Harper Collins Publishers: New York, 1997.

_____. *Fear of Flying*, Henry Holt & Company, Inc.: New York, 1973.

Leonard, Thomas J., *The Portable Coach*, Scribbner: New York, 1998.

Norwood, Robin, *Women Who Love Too Much*, Pocket Books: New York, 1985.

Overeaters Anonymous, *Overeaters Anonymous*, Hazelden Information Education: Torrance, 1980.

Pedersen, Loren E., Ph.D., *Sixteen Men: Understanding Masculine Personality Types,* Shambhala Publications, Inc.: Boston, 1993.

Rand, Ayn, *The Virtue of Selfishness: A New Concept of Egoism*, The New American Library, Inc.: New York, 1961.

Robbins, Anthony, *Unlimited Power*, Simon and Schuster: New York, 1986.

Scantling, Dr. Sandra and Browder, Sue, *Ordinary Women, Extraordinary Sex: Every Woman's Guide to Pleasure and Beyond*, Penguin Books: New York, 1993.

Smothermon, Ron, M.D., *The Man/Woman Book: The Transformation of Love*, Context Publications: San Francisco, 1985.

_____., *Transforming #1*, Context Publications: San Francisco, 1982.

Solomon, Robert C., *About Love: Reinventing Romance for Our Times*, Littlefield Adams Quality Paperbacks: Savage, 1994.

Williams, Paul, *Das Energi*, Warner Books: New York, 1973.

Wurtzel, Elizabeth, *Bitch: In Praise of Difficult Women*, Doubleday: New York, 1998.

Index

Symbols

3 Rís 99

A

abandoned 50
acceptance and denial 119
acknowledgement 7, 128
adult dating 21
adventure 74
affair 65, 95
alienation 117
anchored emotions 109
anchors 104
anger 6, 115
anxiety 109
aphrodisiac 84
appetite 12, 14, 38, 52, 74, 128, 129
appreciation 14
approval 14, 100
approving 64
arousal 85
ascending cycle 7
asking for what you want 24
attraction 65, 70, 133
authenticity 58
availability 69
avoidance 105
avoidance of confrontation 117
avoidance of the truth 105
avoiding intimacy 117
awareness 58

B

baggage 109
biological clock 68
bond 118
boredom 37, 81
boundary 88
brains 99
broken hearts 58
broken homes 58
broken trust 119
business agreement 61
business merger 67

C

challenge 52, 129, 132
change 75
cheating 81
chemistry 61, 69, 71
childbearing years 119
children 64
choice 118
Christianity 72
circular thinking 128
clarity 1, 13, 52
clues 104
co-dependence 110
coldness 116
comfort zone 19, 133
commitment 30, 46, 58, 74, 123, 127
committed level 9
communication 23, 58, 64, 105

A Special Message from the Author

The one thing that clients struggle to achieve is the expression of their appetite. What does appetite mean? How do I know what I want? How do I ask for anything? Isn't it wrong to be so selfish? What about what my man wants? Why do I have to ask for everything?

To assist all of you in refining your appetite and creating distinctions in the expression of it, I welcome you to enroll in my appetite expansion eCourse: "The Expression and Expansion of Appetite in Getting What You Want" on www.relationshipreentry.com.

In that course, I provide specific exercises and tools for you to get clarity about what you really want; practice exercises to become more comfortable learning how to express your appetite, and specific examples of how to ask for the intangible things that all of you desire.

My wish is that women "get it" that they have power in their relationships, much more than they can possibly imagine. Unfortunately, for millions of years, women have been overlooked as a source of energy in this world, and it's about time that someone exposes the pure and powerful source of energy known as a woman's love.

Dear Women:

Your power is feminine and far reaching. If you learn how to use it and channel it effectively, anything that your mind can conceive, you can achieve. Communicate with me. Join my mailing list. Send me your stories, both successes and failures. I welcome your feedback, encouragement, and hearing about your challenges.

I look forward to hearing from you.

Love,
Susan

Susan Sheppard
P.O. Box 251027
Glendale, CA 91209-0404

Susan's Coaching Resources: www.gettingwhatyouwant.com

Dedicated Web Site for this book:
www.howtogetwhatyouwantfromyourmananytime.com

Susan's Relationship Coaching eCourses: www.romancereentry.com

You can order additional copies of this book through iUniverse:
www.iuniverse.com.